THE CRITICS DEBATE

General Editor: Michael Scott

The Critics Debate
General Editor: Michael Scott
Published titles:
Sons and Lovers   Geoffrey Harvey
Bleak House   Jeremy Hawthorn
The Canterbury Tales   Alcuin Blamires
Tess of the d'Urbervilles   Terence Wright
Hamlet   Michael Hattaway
The Waste Land and Ash Wednesday
   Arnold P. Hinchliffe
Paradise Lost   Margarita Stocker
King Lear   Ann Thompson
Othello   Peter Davison
Gulliver's Travels   Brian Tippett
Blake/Songs of Innocence and Experience   David Lindsay
Measure for Measure   T. F. Wharton
The Tempest   David Daniell
Coriolanus   Bruce King
Wuthering Heights   Peter Miles
The Metaphysical Poets   Donald Mackenzie
The Great Gatsby   Stephen Matterson
To the Lighthouse   Su Reid
Heart of Darkness   Robert Barden
**The Portrait of a Lady and The Turn
   of the Screw**   David Kirby

Further titles are in preparation.

THE PORTRAIT OF A LADY

and

THE TURN OF THE SCREW

Henry James and Melodrama

David Kirby

M
MACMILLAN

First published 1991

Published by
MACMILLAN EDUCATION LTD
Houndmills, Basingstoke, Hampshire RG21 2XS
and London
Companies and representatives
throughout the world

Typeset by BP Integraphics Ltd, Bath, Avon
Printed in Hong Kong

British Library Cataloguing in Publication Data
Kirby, David
'The portrait of a lady' and 'The turn of the screw':
Henry James and melodrama. – (The critics debate).
1. Fiction in English. American writers. James, Henry,
1843–1916
I. Title   II. Series
813.4
ISBN 0-333-49237-4
ISBN 0-333-49238-2 pbk

Contents

General Editor's Preface

OVER THE last few years the practice of literary criticism has become hotly debated. Methods developed earlier in the century and before have been attacked and the word 'crisis' has been drawn upon to describe the present condition of English Studies. That such a debate is taking place is a sign of the subject discipline's health. Some would hold that the situation necessitates a radical alternative approach which naturally implies a 'crisis situation'. Others would respond that to employ such terms is to precipitate or construct a false position. The debate continues but it is not the first. 'New Criticism' acquired its title because it attempted something fresh, calling into question certain practices of the past. Yet the practices it attacked were not entirely lost or negated by the new critics. One factor becomes clear: English Studies is a pluralistic discipline.

What are students coming to advanced work in English for the first time to make of all this debate and controversy? They are in danger of being overwhelmed by the cross-currents of critical approaches as they take up their study of literature. The purpose of this series is to help delineate various critical approaches to specific literary texts. Its authors are from a variety of critical schools and have approached their task in a flexible manner. Their aim is to help the reader come to terms with the variety of criticism and to introduce him or her to further reading on the subject and to a fuller evaluation of a particular text by illustrating the way it has been approached in a number of contexts. In the first part of the book a critical survey is given of some of the major ways the text has been appraised. This is done sometimes in a thematic manner, sometimes according to various 'schools' or 'approaches'. In the second part the authors provide their own appraisals of the text from their stated critical standpoint, allowing the reader the knowledge of their own particular approaches from which their views may in turn be evaluated. The series therein hopes to introduce and to elucidate criticism of authors and texts being studied and to encourage participation as the critics debate.

Michael Scott

A Note on Texts and References

Quotations from the novels are taken from the following widely-available texts: *The Portrait of a Lady*, Penguin Classics edition, edited with an introduction by Geoffrey Moore and notes by Patricia Crick (Harmondsworth, 1987); and *The Aspern Papers and The Turn of the Screw*, Penguin Classics edition, edited with an introduction and notes by Anthony Curtis (Harmondsworth, 1987).

For the sake of consistency, when publication dates of James's novels are given, these are the dates of first American editions, exclusive of prepublication or copyright issues and serial publications.

Several of the critical essays in *The Turn of the Screw* section are included in *A Casebook on Henry James's The Turn of the Screw*, edited by Gerald Willen, second edition (New York: Thomas Y. Crowell, 1969), from which quotations are taken for the convenience of the reader, who may wish to consult this single volume rather than the various journals in which the essays appeared originally.

Other works are identified by author and year of publication; full details will be found in the References section.

to Ralph Berry,

Lucan's giant

Isabel Archer may be the fictional heroine above all others with whom modern literary intellectuals are certain to fall in love.

> Harold Bloom, 'Introduction', *Henry James's The Portrait of a Lady* (ed.) Bloom (New York, 1987)

'Well, if I don't know who [the governess] was in love with, I know who *he* was.'

> from the frame story in *The Turn of the Screw*

Introduction

Henry James was called 'the Master' in his lifetime and even to his face. Given such a sobriquet, and given as well the author's acquiescence in the bestowing of it, the reader new to James might well expect to encounter a sort of monster of literature, one of those unapproachable, statue-like writers who seems to be a breed apart, a kind of literary automaton who does nothing but produce books and who has no life outside of the pages he has written.

Yet James had a very rich life. To be sure, it was a life that was almost entirely literary – James had no wife, no lovers, no children, and no profession save that of authorship – yet it was a life marked with exhilarating successes and crushing failures. Indeed, because James's life and his art are so closely linked (though none of his work is overtly autobiographical), it may be more helpful to study the two in tandem than it might be for an author like James's contemporary Mark Twain, for example, even though Twain's life of prospecting and riverboat-piloting was so much more 'adventurous' in the ordinary sense of the term.

James's career has been classified in many ways, from the simple 'early' and 'late' designations to Philip Guedalla's satirical equation of James's periods with the succession of English kings (James the First, James the Second, and James the Old Pretender) to Louis Auchincloss's five-part scheme that concludes with the epoch of 'high, golden light'. In this study, I have chosen to look at the last major work of the early James and the first of the later one – at *The Portrait of a Lady* (1881) and *The Turn of the Screw* (1898), with sufficient reference to the fictions that precede and follow these works to give not only a sense of the author's career as a whole but also an understanding of this key period in James's development. For James, these were 'the theatrical years'; they were marked by great personal suffering, and they are book-ended by two key works – the novel which ended James's first great phase as a writer and the one which inaugurated his final, triumphant phase.

To understand these novels on their own and also in relation to James's personal nightmare, which has at its centre a stagey, starkly-lit moment of public humiliation, one might do well to have recourse to the neglected term 'melodrama'. James actually began his life of writing as an overt melodramatist, heavily influenced by Hawthorne and the Gothic writers of the British tradition, as seen in the early short stories and such novels as *Roderick Hudson* (1875) and *The American* (1877). With the publication of *The Portrait of a Lady*, one of his finest novels (to many critics, *the* finest), James completed what would have amounted to an entire career in the life of almost any other writer. He had published a dozen other volumes in a variety of genres, and *The Portrait of a Lady*, an undisputed masterpiece, represented a culmination of all the lessons he had learned, both from a reading of other authors as well as from the quotidian experience of writing and revising his own work and seeing it in print. More than one critic has noted that *The Portrait of a Lady* is not only an act of homage to the eighteenth- and nineteenth-century novel of realism but also a precursor of the twentieth-century modernist novel with its technical preoccupations; a covert melodrama, *The Portrait of a Lady* has as part of its deep structure the Gothic underpinnings that James doted on as a youthful reader and apprentice writer, yet its foreground is the consciousness of a single character, as would be the case in the novels of Virginia Woolf and William Faulkner. It would have been a perfect book to end a career with.

Instead, James arranged to sabotage himself as surely as if he had thrown himself in front of a runaway carriage. Just as novelists of the present day turn to screenplay writing for the lure of riches or greater fame or the simple urge to do something different, and often at the peril of their sanity and their craft, so James more or less wasted the five years from 1890–1895 writing stilted, unactable plays for the English stage. The theatrical period came to a sickening end on the night of 5 January 1895, when James was mocked by a hostile audience that, as he said, roared at him like beasts in a zoo; in the months that followed, James had what would be called a nervous breakdown today, and the fiction of the next several years (including *The Turn of the Screw*) would be marked by images of captivity, estrangement, powerlessness, suffering and other imaginings of a tormented mind.

Of course, at one level, nothing an author does is time wasted, and the lessons of the theatre made possible new technical advances in James's late fiction, beginning with *The Spoils of Poynton* (1897) and culminating in the great masterpieces of the final period: *The Wings of the Dove* (1902), *The Ambassadors* (1903), and *The Golden Bowl* (1904). Indeed, it would be fair to say that the splendid achievement of the later years would not have been possible had it not been for James's wilful hurling of himself into the personal and professional abyss of the theatre.

But for triumph to rise from failure, James had to re-create himself by going back to his beginnings and, in a very real sense, starting all over again. With *The Turn of the Screw*, James took up once again the pen of the overt melodramatist; with that pen, he revived and fructified his life and art. One is reminded of Dante's *nel mezzo del cammin di nostra vita* and the beginning of the great work in which the artist is lost in a dark wood, yet out of which, after a mighty struggle, he makes his way.

The present study is divided into two halves. The important critical assessments of each book are discussed, and then I present my own views. Every author and every work of literature attracts a different critic and a different form of criticism, of course; thus both *The Portrait of a Lady* and *The Turn of the Screw*, like other James fictions, have occasioned a good many source studies – a prolific author, James was meticulous in recording every detail about the genesis and growth of his work.

But after that, the two texts are treated quite differently by the critics. Specific texts are best served by specific schools of criticism – or if that is not so, at least specific critics seem to think it is. *The Portrait of a Lady*, with its emphasis on theme, character and image, has been of special interest to New Critics because of their propensity for the well-made text, the autonomous literary artifact; this remains true even at the time of this writing, long after the New Criticism has been officially pronounced 'dead'. *The Turn of the Screw*, on the other hand, appeals greatly to psychological critics, since the pre-eminent question is whether the governess who tells the story has a healthy or diseased mind. But just as there are psychological studies of *The Portrait of a Lady* and New Critical readings of *The Turn of the Screw*, so there are many other conceivable approaches from every band in the critical spectrum, and ample if succinct coverage is given to each. No attempt is made here to provide a comprehensive history of twentieth-century criticism, but the reader will be able to track the development of most of the major critical schools as the novels attract the attention of one group of critics and then another. To make this easier, I provide, at appropriate points within each critical section, brief transitional remarks designed to define and otherwise account for the appropriateness of the various schools to James's work.

The critic who has the privilege of building on so rich a heritage of study and debate is like Lucan's pygmy who, placed upon the shoulders of a giant, sees more than the giant himself. Believing as I do that each author demands the single specific critical approach which best illuminates his or her work, I have, while acknowledging the many splendid insights offered by all of my predecessors, decided to approach James as a genre critic would. In a way, each of us is a genre critic before we are anything else, for, upon picking up a book, each of us asks if only implicitly, the same simple question, namely, what has the author written?

The answer, in James's case, is melodrama. In a 1943 essay, Jacques Barzun observed that James is best described as a melodramatist, given his belief that, 'in acting out their feelings, people turn out either good or evil' as well as his 'addiction to violent plots' (p. 509). If melodrama is a depiction of violent interactions between good and evil people, says Barzun, then many works thought of as tragedies would have to be put in the class of melodrama. Tragedy itself is rather narrowly defined, since it implies both a hero and the workings of fate. Thus what do we do with the works 'which lack a magnanimous hero as well as a sense of overriding fate'? We call them melodrama and recognize that tragedy is one of melodrama's subclasses – the highest, Barzun is quick to point out, just as the blood-and-thunder plays of the nineties were the lowest (p. 510).

A number of years would pass before other critics began to use melodrama as an effective tool in James criticism. To date only two full-length studies discuss melodrama in James with any degree of thoroughness. Leo Levy's book provides valuable background discussion; a lengthier and more recent work by Peter Brooks extends Levy's arguments considerably. Brooks has little to say about either *The Portrait of a Lady* or *The Turn of the Screw*, though. And no critic that I have encountered has given sufficient attention to both the conscious and the unconscious use of the language of slavery and imprisonment by James's characters and, to some extent, James himself. It is essential to examine the conscious use of such language in order to understand how these personages view themselves; it is equally essential to examine the unconscious uses in order to see why others may be attracted to these people in the first place – why Isabel might be drawn to Osmond, for example, but why James might be drawn to a character like the governess, so unlike anyone else in the Jamesian canon. Pioneering studies by Stuart Culver and Mark Seltzer deal with the attractions of power and authority in James's art and life; much more remains to be done in this area.

To see James as a melodramatist is to see him both as a literary historian (his emphasis on the importance of literary sources in his own writing makes that clear) as well as a seeker after truth and power in a world without fixed values. Not only does melodrama accurately define James's writing, then, but it also connects at one end to the oldest form of scholarship, which is source-hunting, and, at the other, to the latest applications of Freudian and Marxist theory.

To my teachers Donald Stanford and Charles Anderson and to colleagues and students too numerous to name I offer my heartfelt thanks for their aid in appreciating the life and work of Henry James. Thanks as well to Will Kirby for invaluable editorial assistance. During the last twenty years, I have stood on many a shoulder; the sturdiest of these belong to the polymath and *bon vivant* Ralph Berry, to whom this volume is dedicated.

The Portrait of a Lady

Part One:
Survey

1 Source criticism

To study literary influence is to encounter two dominant opinions on
the matter: one, argued largely by scholars, decries the significance of
influence altogether, while the other, voiced largely by writers themselves, cheerfully admits to wholesale borrowings from contempor-
aries as well as forebears. Virtually all of the source studies of *The
Portrait of a Lady* argue that James began with a particular literary
source but then built upon and improved on it or, at the very least,
changed the source material to suit his own purposes. The greatest
number of source studies revolve around James's debt to George
Eliot, but the earliest sources appear to be drawn from fictions by
authors of much less renown. For example, Andrea Roberts Beauchamp argues convincingly that one source may have been a brief
didactic tale entitled 'Isabel Archer' that appeared in a popular
family magazine during James's youth (1977). While there is no
evidence for James having read the story, which was written by
someone known to posterity only as 'Professor Alden, D. D.' and
which was published in the 1848–49 volume of *The Ladies' Wreath*,
there are striking parallels between it and James's novel. In Alden's
four-page story, a country-fresh Isabel Archer comes to New York
and, though reluctant to marry, finds herself succumbing to a
polished gentleman who later turns out to be 'unkind, irreligious,
ruined' (p. 270). The difference between the two fictions is that
Alden's Isabel remains mired in a miserable marriage, thus serving
as a warning to other naive young women, whereas James's heroine
pursues a much more complex destiny.

A second study traces the connection between *The Portrait of a Lady*
and the Gothic tradition that played so important a role in James's
early reading, as will be argued in the Appraisal section of the present

study. Elsa Nettels observes that the eighteenth-century Gothic romance, which has its origin in Horace Walpole's *The Castle of Otranto* (1765) and which reached its peak in the novels of Ann Radcliffe, was highly influential in the careers of English and American novelists of the nineteenth and twentieth centuries. Generally, these later writers approached the Gothic romance in one of two ways: either they burlesqued or parodied Gothic conventions (examples include Jane Austen's *Northanger Abbey* (1818), Thomas Love Peacock's *Nightmare Abbey* (1818), and some of the tales of Irving and Poe) or else they transcended the conventional uses of Gothic elements and gave those elements moral and psychological dimensions. In Emily Brontë's *Wuthering Heights* (1847), Herman Melville's *Moby-Dick* (1851), and Nathaniel Hawthorne's *The Scarlet Letter* (1850), for example, characters and other plot elements have symbolic and mythic importance beyond their surface values and thus resonate with, not merely dramatic reality, but psychological reality as well.

James was fascinated 'by the Gothic novelists' favorite themes of imprisonment, possession, exploitation, and deception' and generally followed the path of the second group of writers in his novels, although in *The Portrait of a Lady* he actually uses Gothic conventions in both ways (p. 73). Were he to simply assimilate the Gothic novel, Isabel would be engaged to Lord Warburton, kidnapped by Merle and Osmond, and escape from them to marry the English peer. Instead, the novel uses Gothic imagery to show how Isabel is self-deceived; this burlesquing takes place mainly in the celebrated vigil scene in Chapter 42, where the images all rise from the mind of Isabel. The transcendence of the Gothic mode takes place when Isabel goes back to rescue Pansy, who, as Isabel was, is on the marriage market – that is, on the brink of a disastrous liaison. In the last part of the novel, the reader sees Isabel grow through suffering. With conventional Gothic heroines, 'simply the removal of the physical danger assures relief', but 'if James were to permit Isabel at the end to escape Osmond and find happiness with Goodwood or another, he would shift the emphasis from the true subject of the novel and undermine the validity of everything portrayed before' (p. 81).

The James-Eliot connection was first trumpeted by F. R. Leavis, who, with typical bravado, announced, 'Henry James wouldn't have written *The Portrait of a Lady* if he hadn't read *Gwendolyn Harleth* (as I shall call the good part of *Daniel Deronda*), and of the pair of closely comparable works, George Eliot's has not only the distinction of

having come first; it is decidedly the greater' (p. 85). Leavis suggests
this is so because 'Isabel Archer is Gwendolyn Harleth seen by a
man. And it has to be added that, in presenting such a type, George
Eliot has a woman's advantage' (p. 86). More than one reader of *The
Portrait of a Lady* has complained that, except for a few isolated instances, we learn precious little concerning the actual workings of Isabel's
mind; Leavis too faults James in this area but, in so doing, offers
a backhanded compliment that almost outweighs the criticism:
'James's marvelous art is devoted to contenting us with very little in
the way of inward realization of Isabel, and to keep us interested,
instead, in a kind of psychological detective work – keeping us intently
wondering from the outside, and constructing, on a strict economy of
evidence, what is going on inside' (p. 110). It is important to note that
Leavis does not prefer the whole of *Daniel Deronda* (1874) to the James
novel, only what he calls *Gwendolyn Harleth* or the part devoted to the
development of the character he sees as the basis for Isabel Archer.

Leavis's comments have occasioned a good many replies, the best
of which feature elaborations of Leavis's often-blunt assertions as
well as genuine quarrels with his basic premises. One contributor to
the James-Eliot debate believes that the true basis for Isabel Archer
is not Gwendolyn Harleth but Dorothea Brooke of *Middlemarch*
(1871). According to George Levine, one main difference between the
two Eliot characters is that Gwendolyn Harleth, who must either
marry Henleigh Grandcourt or become a governess, has no real
freedom, whereas Dorothea Brooke has the kind of freedom from
ordinary economic pressures that Isabel Archer has. On the other
hand, something that the two Eliot heroines have in common is that
the 'bad husband' of each dies. James does not take this way out and
therefore seems to be saying that 'the mistake once made is in some
sense irrevocable. The meaning of Isabel's life becomes entirely inter-
nal and can never find expression in action. Her dignity is silent and
miserable' (p. 256). Eliot approaches and then backs away from the
grim admission that society is incurable and the individual must live
for herself alone, says Levine, while James embraces it.

Robert Emmet Long breaks new ground in the dispute about
sources by arguing that while James found his starting point in *Daniel
Deronda*, he completed his portrait with the aid of materials provided
by his American master, Nathaniel Hawthorne. The method of Hawthorne allowed James to limit his central character yet study her all
the more intensely. The Hawthorne novel that is most important in

this respect is *The Marble Faun* (1860), which, like *The Portrait of a Lady*, treats the theme of American innocence confronting experience in an Italian garden setting. But in 'improving' upon Eliot, James improves upon Hawthorne as well. James's interest in *The Portrait of a Lady* is 'the delineation of character as it evolves through social experience. How different from Hawthorne, whose characters have only a vague social identity, and do not expand, is James's portrait of Isabel Archer, which requires hundreds of pages to execute, and is not completed until, on the last page, her final gesture is made'. (p. 116).

A final article cites another source altogether – not, however, in a manner which refutes Leavis *et al.* but which, instead, reveals how a great work will not only combine but transcend a variety of sources. While allowing that *Daniel Deronda* and other novels figure into the making of *The Portrait of a Lady*, Joseph L. Tribble has written a well-researched and convincing essay which points to Victor Cherbuliez's *Le Roman d'une Honnête Femme* (1866) as the primary source of the James novel. Cherbuliez's plot alone substantiates Tribble's argument: Isabel de Loanne is rescued from a provincial life by the Baroness de Ferjeux, who marries Isabel off to her nephew, the Marquis de Lestang. Like Gilbert Osmond, the Marquis is a connoisseur who chooses Isabel as he would a work of art, i.e., to reflect his own good taste; too, he has had a secret lover, a Madame Mirveil. Nonetheless, a disillusioned Isabel resolves to live with her husband, to keep up appearances and not give him the satisfaction of seeing her weaken, and even though a suitor named Arsene Dolfin begs her to flee with him, she returns to the Marquis at the end. It is then that the only major divergence from James's plot occurs, for unlike Isabel Archer, Isabel de Loanne is thrilled to discover that her husband has really loved her all along.

As usual, James has expanded on his source material; the Cherbuliez novel is but seventy-three pages and contains four major characters, whereas *The Portrait of a Lady* runs to 312 pages in the edition used by Tribble and features ten major characters. More important, 'the plot of James's novel is more complex, and yet more realistic: the melodramatic incidents are eliminated, the various parts are more skilfully integrated into the whole, and the conclusion is much more in keeping with the action that precedes it,' which is enough to convince Tribble that '*Daniel Deronda* may have helped James to see the weaknesses in *Le Roman d'une Honnête Femme*, but

George Eliot's novel did not displace what his imagination had found there' (pp. 292–3).

Thus the source studies of *The Portrait of a Lady* do not, as they might easily, fall out into a chaos of charges and counter-charges. Instead, subsequent studies build on previous ones in a way which demonstrates how the creative mind works at its best. A true literary masterpiece like *The Portrait of a Lady* draws on a variety of sources yet transcends them so completely that it seems, to all but the most careful critical eye, entirely 'original'.

2 Textual criticism

If the source critic assumes that the author derived his ideas and images from some earlier text, the textual critic tries to determine what steps the author took in order to constitute an authoritative or final text of his own. Almost all of James's novels appear in three forms: first in a serialized magazine appearance, then as a first-edition book, and finally as a volume in the 1907 New York Edition of his collected works. Many of these novels were revised hastily between their first and second appearances, and a number of the earlier ones underwent extensive revision for the New York Edition. The result is, according to some critics, a clash of styles. For example, *The American*, written in the relatively simpler style of 1877, is seen by some readers as marred by the more orotund phrasings added by James when he revised it more than thirty years later.

This is not so much of a problem with *The Portrait of a Lady*, since by the time of its composition James had already taken up his mature style. Thus most of the textual studies of *The Portrait of a Lady* deal less with the matter of the novel being improved or damaged and more with fundamental changes in structure and character development.

One reader has discovered a succinct revision that may nonetheless affect one's understanding of the entire novel. In revising *The Portrait of a Lady* for the New York Edition, says Anthony J. Mazzella (1972), James found that the novel would be published in two volumes (it had originally appeared as one), cutting it roughly in half. Since the first volume would end with Chapter 27, which was already roughly parallel to the final chapter, James took the opportunity to further revise the earlier chapter so that both volumes would conclude with similar gestures, dialogue and plot development. In the concluding chapter to each volume, a rejected suitor is removed from the action (in Chapter 27, it's Lord Warburton) and Isabel is left alone with Gilbert Osmond. The result is a doubling of the idea that Isabel chooses Osmond freely and in full knowledge of the alternatives.

In addition to studies like this one which examine brief, dramatic revisions, there are others concerned with extensive, page-by-page revisions that result in the alteration of Isabel Archer's character. Nina Baym states forthrightly that James's heroine 'appears on almost every page of the book, and virtually every page about her undergoes change. Although some of these are only excisions or substitutions of single words, the cumulative effect is considerable' (p. 185). The chief intent of these changes is to give Isabel a rich mental life and the subtle consciousness required for a late James heroine.

If the early Isabel is trapped by her simplicity, the late one is victimized by Osmond's and Madame Merle's appeal to her higher faculties. This progress from fool to saint is signalled by heightened language: 'brilliant and noble' (1881) becomes 'high and splendid ... and yet oh so radiantly gentle!' (1908), and 'a bright spirit' is revised as 'a "lustre" beyond any recorded losing or rediscovering'. With the increased emphasis on Isabel, there is a corresponding loss of importance on the part of the minor characters; 'when he is through', writes Baym, 'James has left nothing solid for the reader except the boundless imagination of Isabel. But in 1881 a limited imagination is her greatest shortcoming' (p. 185). The revised *The Portrait of a Lady* is a clouded and problematical work to Baym. The early *The Portrait of a Lady* argued that awareness would lead to independence, whereas the late one says that independence is obtainable only through awareness – the points are almost identical, with the difference being that awareness ceases to be a means for Isabel and becomes an end. To achieve this, James had to sacrifice formal perfection in order to create a wiser, subtle Isabel.

Mazzella (1975) too examines the many revisions involving the character of Isabel Archer; while he would seem to agree with Baym's assertions regarding the heightened consciousness of the late Isabel, he notes another subtle but important difference between the two heroines. The late Isabel 'is only dimly aware – unlike the first Isabel who is not aware at all – that the basis of her anxiety is fear that the freedom constituted by the clear conduct of her consciousness may be annihilated by sexual possession.' In all, the revised *The Portrait of a*

Lady is 'a study . . . of the life of the mind of the later Isabel' whereas the original was 'frequently an uneven portrait of a girl's caprice'; moreover, this girl 'does what she does for reasons perhaps best ascribed to the folly of her youth and the esthetics of her incompleteness' (p. 619). Throughout his essay, Mazzella suggests that James's identity is related inextricably to the mature character of Isabel Archer, that her altered state reflects the novelist's sense of his own fully developed consciousness as well as his squeamishness about sex.

3 Technical and structural criticism

In a general sense, it would be perfectly logical to discuss literary uses of technique and structure separately. Students of technique look at the minutiae of method, such as an author's use of point of view, while students of structure look at relations of a given work's large parts, as one might ponder the acts of a play. But I have combined technical and structural criticism into a single category here because James's own practice seems to require it, as numerous critics have discovered. In James, *how* a character sees determines *what* she sees in its totality.

Thus, there are a number of lengthy and complex essays dealing with both James's use of sophisticated narrative technique in *The Portrait of a Lady* and the resultant elaborate structure of the novel. Throughout his career, and increasingly so from the middle period onward, James prided himself as an architect of the novel; in the critical Prefaces to the New York Edition, he refers to himself implicitly and, on occasion, explicitly as an architect or engineer, a master builder who is not only constructing impressive edifices but also bequeathing to posterity a set of plans that others may adopt for their own purposes. In addition, *The Portrait of a Lady* is a transitional novel in James's career and in the development of the novel as a whole. Therefore, its specific historical importance combined with James's general desire to be a literary theorist as well as practitioner make the novel an object of crucial interest to students of James's writing. Technical-structural studies of *The Portrait of a Lady* make it clear that to understand technique is to understand the real meaning of James's novels. And to some extent, to understand technique is to understand James himself, given the emphasis, in the Prefaces, that he places on the operation of his own critical sensibilities.

David Daiches calls *The Portrait of a Lady* 'the first of James's full-length novels to illustrate clearly and successfully what he was trying to achieve in his fiction' (p. 573). He makes his point by contrasting *The Portrait of a Lady* to *Roderick Hudson*. The latter is an old-fashioned 'novel of public significance' in which physical and moral events are equated, often unconvincingly; thus Roderick has to get drunk at Baden-Baden to signify his moral failure as man and artist, and he tests the reader's credulousness by becoming engaged to Mary Garland so that he can further endanger his soul when he proves unfaithful to her (p. 574).

The Portrait of a Lady, on the other hand, is a ground-breaking 'novel of personal sensibility' in which important occurrences, notably Isabel's decision to return to Osmond, are presented as decisions rather than mere events (p. 573). What makes the difference between the 'life' portrayed in *Roderick Hudson* and the 'felt life' of *The Portrait of a Lady* and most of the fiction that followed it? Technique, says Daiches: 'style, structure, organization' is the 'filter that distinguishes "life" from "felt life"' (p. 577). Writing in 1943, Daiches felt that 'full justice has not yet been done to James as a writer whose technical skill enabled him to make convincing and inevitable a personal moral interpretation of human behavior – in other words, as a novelist of sensibility' (p. 579). This observation was made just before the great post-war surge in literary studies, and while the nature of interpretation precludes there ever being a so-called last word on any author, the concluding portion of this section will make clear how sophisticated literary analysis has become since Daiches' day.

In 'The Art of Fiction' (1884), James chides Anthony Trollope for admitting in his fictional digressions that, as a novelist, he was only pretending, only practising the art of make-believe, and thereby suggesting that the novelist is less interested in truth than the historian. Linda A. Westervelt notes that James refers to *The Portrait of a Lady* (completed three years before he wrote 'The Art of Fiction') as a 'history' and uses that term in the text seven times; to her, James's desire to be a historian not only resulted in a technical shift within the novel but also a development in literary history, since *The Portrait of a Lady* 'opens with the conventions of a Victorian novel but ends as a modern one' (p. 74). Specifically, James stops using the intrusive, omniscient Victorian narrator halfway through and instead adopts the manner of a historian and begins to treat Isabel as a real person. The upshot of this technical experiment is nothing less than the

modern novel itself, 'with ambiguous circumstances, direct presenta-
tion of character, and the resulting increased participation of the
reader' (p. 75). Readers need to remember that although James is
said to have perfected his centre of consciousness technique in *The
Portrait of a Lady*, he does not do so until the novel is nearly finished;
the shift in technique makes it necessary for Isabel to become the
central consciousness by the time of her meditative vigil in Chapter
42, the part of the book of which James was justifiably so proud.

Too, the novelist-as-historian idea means that Isabel must accept
the testimony of the otherwise frivolous and unreliable Countess
Gemini regarding Pansy's parentage, whereas in a Trollope novel,
the narrative rather than a character would have related these facts.
Again, though, James is inventing not only the modern novel and the
modern character but the modern reader as well: 'What is true for
Isabel – that she knows only by impressions – beomes true for the
reader as well' (p. 83).

While it may seem somewhat anomalous to describe a novel written in the 1880s as modern when that term is more often associated
with the work of writers such as Eliot and Pound, the fact that Isabel
'knows only by impressions' does indeed suggest the fragmented consciousness portrayed by the great modernist masters. According to
Sheldon W. Liebman, point of view is not merely of technical importance in *The Portrait of a Lady*; it becomes the subject of the novel as
well. Or rather it is points of view that are stressed, with James
exploiting the inevitable tensions that result from conflicting out-
looks. The theme of point of view is introduced early in a conversation
between Isabel Archer and Lord Warburton's two sisters in which
Isabel accuses the radically-inclined yet wealthy peer of a false 'position' and is informed by the Misses Molyneux that their brother's
'position' is one of the finest in the land; that the heroine is speaking of
a moral stance and the other characters of a social one suggests that
words have multiple meanings, that communication is inherently
difficult, and that different points of view are very likely to collide.

Beyond this thematic significance, though, point of view is also
used by James as a structural device to emphasize the problems
inherent in the development of Isabel's character. Even though
Isabel is the novel's centre of consciousness, she is affected by the
points of view of the other characters. The phrase itself is used with
some frequency: for example, the reader is told that Henrietta
Stackpole wants to write journalism 'from the American point of

view', and later Mrs Touchett tells Henrietta that 'We judge from different points of view'. When Isabel and her aunt discuss the subject, Isabel says that her point of view, like Henrietta's, is American, whereas Mrs Touchett responds that there are as many points of view in the world as there are people and that her own is intensely personal, an outlook which is central to an understanding of the novel, according to Liebman, and one to which he alludes at the conclusion of his essay (p. 137).

In the meantime, the great bulk of the novel is shot through with one misunderstanding after another; just as the phrase 'point of view' is used throughout, so is 'I don't understand' or some version thereof. After three years of marriage, Osmond tells Isabel that she does not understand him, and indeed she does not. 'She discovers, at last, the validity of Mrs Touchett's epigram – that points of view are as numerous as the people who have them. She learns to see, also, that points of view are not one – but multi-dimensional, and that any position has its advantages and disadvantages' (p. 147). The result is, if not happiness, at least a knowledge that yields understanding and sympathy.

In fact, if James were to define happiness in *The Portrait of a Lady*, he would almost certainly equate it with limited consciousness, since a mature sensibility can only be aware of the world's moral and spiritual impoverishment. And given the type of novel that he wanted to write, it seems that the inevitable result would have to be tragic, given James's own gloomy assessment of the times he lived in. Charles Feidelson believes that the Preface to the New York Edition of *The Portrait of a Lady* reveals 'the recessive and dominant strains in James's notion of himself and his art', the former being to emphasize other characters' views of Isabel and create a traditional social novel and the latter emphasizing Isabel's own consciousness (p. 49). However, the resultant work of fiction portrays neither a passive heroine fatally enmeshed in a restrictive social order nor an active one who reshapes her world but someone who moves between the two positions and with disastrous results. 'Beginning as social comedy and modulating into a sort of comedy of triumphant consciousness', *The Portrait of a Lady* soon becomes something else entirely, its comedy giving way to 'a tale of an evil fate' (p. 52). The novel changes when Osmond and Madame Merle enter, for like Ralph Touchett, Henrietta Stackpole, Warburton and Goodwood, they represent a declining social order, but unlike them, they fed on the decay and grow stronger. No matter how much Isabel's consciousness expands, it takes on an unmanageable task when it moves from a world of feckless suitors to Osmond's world, and the result is pathos. If the novel's ending is tragically heroic, it is because Isabel's decision to return to Osmond is inconclusive in a manner that is all but fatal.

If *The Portrait of a Lady* seems unusually problematic, it is because of the ambitious (some readers would say over-ambitious) task that its author set for himself. Joyce's *Ulysses* (1922) may be more complex technically than *The Portrait of a Lady*, but while Joyce seems to find formal liberation within the confines of a single twenty-four hour day, Henry James must confront the fact that his arena, that is, his heroine's consciousness, is essentially boundless. The absence of limits means the absence of helpful guidelines and signposts as well; at least the action of *Ulysses* is impelled forward by the passage of time and such quotidian occurrences as the serving of meals, the openings and closings of pubs, and so on. One of the aspects of composition that has most fascinated critics is the way in which James compensated for his technical ambition and, along the way, changed the nature of the novel altogether. One such compensation, according to Martha Collins, is the decreasing interference of the narrator as the novel progresses and as James's career progresses as well. For if the narrator's most extensive analysis of Isabel takes place in Chapter 6 and then falls off swiftly thereafter, so too do narrators figure less as analysts in the later novels, with the result that the reader is compelled to interpret a character like Lambert Strether of *The Ambassadors* in a way that he does not interpret the heroine of *The Portrait of a Lady*.

As Isabel's consciousness grows, the narrator's role decreases, as do the roles of Ralph Touchett and the other male satellites who provide perspective; 'as Isabel moves from self-absorption, to interested but faulty observation, to enlightened awareness of others, she gradually emerges as a reliable center of consciousness, displacing both the narrator and the satellites'; the final focus is not on a fixed group of characters in a social milieu but on the heroine's 'fluid mind' (p. 156). Clearly Collins is one of those readers who is not disturbed by James's Emersonian indifference to a foolish consistency and for whom technical anomalies are equivalent to psychological realities.

4 New criticism (image)

Following the arguments of the technical-structural critics, with their often-contentious emphasis on authorial manipulation, it is with some relief that one turns to the so-called New Critics. Facetiously yet truthfully referred to as the lemon-squeezing school of literary criticism, the New Criticism ruthlessly excludes the author's declared intentions and all other extratextual considerations and instead looks only at the text and its component parts, examining those parts within the context of the work itself and only in that context. A complement to the purely historical criticism of the source and textual critics as well as an antidote to purely impressionistic reactions to literature, the New Criticism had its origin in close readings of lyric poetry; for that reason, in its purest form the New Criticism is concerned largely with images and symbols. As will be seen, however, later critics extended the application of New Critical techniques to character and theme as well.

Among studies of imagery, Charles R. Anderson's *Person, Place and Thing in Henry James* is both a culmination of previous findings as well as a seminal work for present and future critics. Anderson argues that James breaks new ground in fiction by having his characters understand themselves and each other by means of images which have first one meaning and then another. In his chapter on *The Portrait of a Lady*, Anderson focuses on the ambivalent meaning of the word 'vista', which he calls 'the controlling word of the novel' and one that is usually employed by James in the Italian sense of a panorama. There is another meaning to 'vista', however, an English meaning that denotes the convergence of one's vision, according to the laws of perspective, on some object, generally an object of beauty. In the celebrated forty-second chapter, the image is given both its meanings simultaneously and with crushing irony when Isabel, reflecting on Osmond's villainy, finds 'the infinite vista of a multiplied life to be a dark, narrow alley, with a dead wall at the end – no statue or fountain there to take the eye with beauty' (p. 91).

Anderson examines retrospective meditations from *Pride and Prejudice* (1813) and *The Scarlet Letter* (1850) to show that other authors have used such scenes for commentary or for accelerated narration, though Austen and Hawthorne's meditations tend to be brief and to shed light on a single past episode. In contrast, James's is a full-scale meditation, lasting a chapter, and it reviews the entire novel. Anderson counts the giving of multiple meanings to a central image and the extension of the possibilities of the retrospective meditation among James's key contributions to modernist fiction and notes that these effects can be seen in Conrad's *Heart of Darkness* (1902), Joyce's *Ulysses* and Faulkner's *Absalom, Absalom!* (1936).

Whereas the technical-structural critics often equate the success (or failure) of James as a writer with the believability of Isabel as a character, the New Critics tend to separate author from heroine and emphasize the irony inherent in the contrast between James's knowing artistry and Isabel Archer's self-delusion. For example, Viola Hopkins Winner examines a whole category of skilfully-handled architectural and related images that demonstrate how Isabel failed to understand the unfolding of her destiny. When Madame Merle tells Isabel that there is no such thing as an isolated man or woman and that one must take into account a person's 'whole envelope of circumstances' (meaning his or her house, clothes, possessions and friends), Isabel disagrees initially (p. 140). But the novel is written so as to show Madame Merle to be right. Houses are especially important: the house in Albany, where Isabel reads about but does not experience life; Gardencourt, the very name of which implies harmony between civilization and nature; Osmond's high, windowless villa in Florence; and the palazzo in Rome, a structure that resembles a fortress or prison.

Possessions and how one uses them matter, too: both Ralph and Gilbert are intellectually subtle and civilized, but whereas Ralph wears his culture lightly, 'Osmond exemplifies the museum consciousness at its worst; his relation to the past is arbitrary, artificial, and lifeless' (p. 140). By returning to Osmond at the end, Isabel shows that she understands and, in a way, agrees with Madame Merle's statement and that therefore she must not try to deny her circumstances. But whereas Osmond and Merle insist inflexibly that one's 'whole envelope of circumstances' is more important, Isabel knows better – that circumstances do count, but the self is primary. If the net seems to tighten around her at the end, she still has more choices than the other characters; thus the novel's title, despite what some readers believe, 'is not meant to be commiserative. Isabel is not trapped within a frame. In accepting the limitations of a frame, she becomes in herself, in her acceptance of the imperfect world in its materiality, a representation of the ideal in the real, which is what James looked for in great portraiture' (p. 143).

In addition to the commentaries by Anderson on vistas and Winner on houses, there are a number of essays dealing with the related idea of window and door images, images which also define Isabel's vision and freedom of movement. For example, John Rodenbeck makes much of James's fascination with the young Isabel in the study of her

Albany house. Here Isabel is described as being very close to the
street but having no desire to look into it and destroy the illusion that
'there was a strange, unseen place on the other side – a place which
became, to the child's imagination, according to its different moods, a
region of delight or of terror'. James is careful to describe Isabel's
imagination here, says Rodenbeck, so that the reader can see how that
imagination accounts for her suffering in the second half of the novel
and, in the end, for her new sense of life. Of Isabel's imagination
James says, 'when the door was not open it jumped out of the window' (p. 331), and both images figure significantly in the novel's
development; the sequestered Pansy, for instance, promises Osmond
that she will not pass through the door of his house. At the end, having
gone out by the window of the imagination for so long, Isabel bursts
through the door of imprisonment that Osmond has bolted against
her, and if she doesn't mean to let Goodwood through, as he hopes, at
least she intends never to let Osmond close it again.

There are, of course, significant images in *The Portrait of a Lady*
besides the ones that apply primarily to Isabel. Paul O. Williams
analyses an image used by Osmond to describe his relationship to
Isabel and finds multiple meanings. In Chapter 47, Osmond says to
Caspar Goodwood, 'We're as united, you know, as the candlestick
and the snuffers'. First of all, because of its sexual nature, the image is
intended to taunt Goodwood, who would have ground his teeth had
he understood, although the innuendo seems to pass right over his
head – a fact that the superior-feeling Osmond can exult in. Secondly,
this image expresses Osmond's own ironic awareness that his relationship with Isabel is one of struggle and opposition rather than
harmony. Finally, however, the reader alone will be aware that,
through its association with other light-dark images in the novel, this
image suggests that Isabel is the active principle in the marriage
whereas Osmond is the passive one, the mere preserver of domestic
order, as befits one who is described by his wife as having 'a genius
for upholstery' (Chapter 38). Thus this key image reveals both
Osmond's attitudes and his blindness to his own deficiencies.

It often seems that, no matter where it begins, sooner or later every
critical road leads to Chapter 42 of *The Portrait of a Lady* with its
depiction of Isabel's midnight vigil. Technically, thematically, and of
course, imagistically, that chapter sums up all that has gone before
and makes ready the way of the future, both in the sense of this
particular novel and in the sense of the development of novelistic form

generally. The author himself had some sense of the chapter's significance; John T. Frederick observes that 'only once, in his careful
preparation of the "Prefaces" for the New York Edition of his work,
did Henry James single out a specific chapter of one of his novels
for definite commendation' (p. 150). In Chapter 42, three patterns
of imagery suggesting imprisonment/freedom, darkness/light, and
cold/heat are thoroughly integrated into Isabel's step-by-step realization of the precise nature of her marriage to Osmond. The three
types of images are used implicitly but also explicitly (as when a
servant brings fresh candles that are later observed to have burned
down to their sockets), and they come together in the final paragraph
as Isabel sits in what she has realized earlier is 'the house of darkness,
the house of dumbness, the house of suffocation' (p. 156) and feels the
room growing dark and chilly around her.

5   New criticism (character)

A second group of New Critics applies to the characters of this novel
the technique of close reading and of linking one aspect of a text to
another in order to create a reading that is a unified and highly-
charged whole; predictably, the results vary, which is to say that the
critics' views of Isabel Archer and her satellites vary. In one of the
best guides to James's development as a novelist, Philip M.
Weinstein looks at six of the fictions, using *The Portrait of a Lady* as the
fulcrum on which the writer's career turned. Before, two separate
modes of living were depicted, vision and action; after, the two modes
are combined. In *Roderick Hudson*, for example, vision and action are
embodied roughly in the characters of Rowland Mallet and Roderick
Hudson respectively. In *The Portrait of a Lady*, the two modes are
'uneasily blended' in Isabel Archer, resulting in a character who is, if
richly drawn, also somewhat confusing (p. 3).

James solved his characterization problem in the later novels
because by then his attitude toward the life of the imagination had
changed, for while Rowland Mallet and Isabel are more or less tragically condemned to an imaginative life only, Lambert Strether of *The
Ambassadors* tragicomically accepts the imaginative life as more desirable than the active one. The key that opens the door to the second
half of James's career is the meditation in Chapter 42, which appeared exceptional in *The Portrait of a Lady* and then became the norm
in the later works.

Invariably, students of Isabel's character agree with the rich-but-confusing verdict, although they disagree as to which adjective should be emphasized over the other. Daniel Schneider's study of character in James begins with Ezra Pound's belief that critics have neglected James's hatred of oppression and his depiction, in book after book, of the individual struggle against bondage in all its forms. To Schneider, each of James's main characters is a divided self, part of whom is passive and seeks merely to avoid oppressors and part of whom resists the bullying and fights fiercely for independence. Thus Isabel is triumphant, but only if one suspends the usual stereotypes, because to succeed in James's world is to be free rather than happy, and if Isabel is not happy in the usual sense at the end, she is certainly free (as readers often observe, she could have gone away with Goodwood or done any number of other things).

Isabel may appear to be a loser to some because she does not acquire, conquer and manage the way Osmond does, but Osmond, like the other collectors in James's fiction, is trapped by all he has acquired, conquered and managed – including, ironically, Isabel. Besides, acquisition, conquest and management are not the goals; freedom is. When Isabel realizes the truth about her marriage in the night-long meditation scene, she frees herself from illusion. Then, at the end, when she returns to what she knows is stifling, even evil, she is nonetheless free from it because her knowledge of it is now complete. She might have entered into an attachment with Caspar Goodwood, but she is truly free for the first time in her life; so instead of sinking passively into a relationship with him, she decides to pursue actively the freedom she has just discovered.

Sheldon W. Liebman describes a sort of dance that takes place between Isabel and pairs of subordinate characters, a dance that allows her to achieve her full potential as she begins provincially and ends fully realized. In each pair there is a suitor and his female confidante: Caspar Goodwood and Henrietta Stackpole, Lord Warburton and Mrs Touchett, Gilbert Osmond and Madame Merle. The first pair is characterized by vitality of spirit, the third by formal graciousness (the second represents an unsatisfactory combination of those qualities). In the process of stepping from partner to partner, Isabel moves to 'a final stage of moral, aesthetic, and psychological superiority, having acquired through experience, knowledge, and through knowledge, virtue' (pp. 178–9).

Not all critics view Isabel's character so positively, of course. The reader who pays attention to the narrator's opinions rather than those of the heroine's friends and satellites will see her as prideful and impatient rather than morally and intellectually superior, according to Robert W. Stallman. Osmond, too, is misread. He is cold and selfish but not evil, as most critics have made him out to be (for that matter, Isabel is cold and selfish, too, says Stallman); again, the problem is that the reader takes his cues from the friends and satellites of Isabel, who despise Osmond, and not from the more objective narrator. Perhaps a better way to see them is as realist and romantic, with Osmond as 'the realist undermining the presumptuous fixed ideas of our romantic heroine' (p. 30). By the end of the novel, they seem ideal for each other – when this 'pretentious, imperceptive, and self-deluded heroine' (p. 32) goes back to Rome, it is because she realizes that she must adhere to 'the social code of appearances, conformity, resignation' (p. 31) that Osmond represents. There is one completely hateful character, of course. Madame Merle manipulates both Isabel and Osmond to ensure Pansy a financial, social and marital future.

In response to the broadsides of Stallman and similar-minded critics, Harriet Blodgett shows how James uses clue after clue to assert what to him is important: that Isabel Archer will become and then behave as a lady, that is, 'an aristocrat of the spirit' (p. 27). To some readers, Isabel may appear cold, but James 'evidently wished to portray . . . the strength possible in a woman who is not motivated by her sexuality but rather by her principles and asexual affections, and would take care to emphasize that intention when he revised the book' (p. 34). If, in fact, 'James looked at women as a woman, not a man, might do, namely, as if they were persons, not sexual objects', and since, 'contemporary with *Portrait*, James was objecting [in his essays] to sexual portraits of women as reductive', then '*Portrait* gives sufficient reason to assume that Isabel Archer is James's tribute to the woman who can operate her ideals' (p. 34). Isabel is repeatedly associated with a Coreggio painting of a Virgin kneeling before a delightful infant, to cite but one of the clues which shows that Isabel is both rendered asexual and idealized.

Perhaps the strongest defence of Isabel Archer's character is one that takes into account her fatal flaw and strongest link with Osmond, namely, her love of appearances. But to think that James was more critical of Isabel than approving is to drain the book of its tragic meaning, writes Dorothea Krook, and 'diminish almost out of existence Isabel Archer's stature as a tragic heroine' (p. 41). The struggle between the love of appearances and the love of truth and reality is a major theme in many James novels, and in them, as *The Portrait of a Lady*, 'the destructive element is always and insistently shown as the obverse of a nature essentially good – essentially generous, passionate and disinterested' (p. 44). Or, as the dying Ralph Touchett says to Isabel, a mistake as generous as hers can only hurt a little.

Indeed, Isabel's complex characterization is consistent with the tragic form and not otherwise, for tragedy presumes that the hero or heroine is to some extent culpable. The genre presumes as well that the villain is more than a mere brute, which is why Osmond, like Isabel, is more guilty of misjudgment than of any worse crime. Money is important to him, and so is the collector's instinct to possess Isabel, but he likes her, too – he finds her charming and graceful and falls in love to the extent he can. Overall, the tragedy hangs on his dislike of her ideas, specifically her moral objections to the degenerate mores of Roman society (to which Osmond wants desperately to belong). Krook notes that this is 'one of the profoundest of the tragic ironies of life: to be rejected and despised ... for what is best in one, and by those in whom one has placed one's most loving trust' (p. 56). In the end, it is Isabel's fatal aestheticism, her love of appearances, which is her deepest bond with Osmond. It is this that sends her back to him.

Edward Wagenknecht has managed to sit out the storm of vilification and praise by seeking shelter in a Keatsian negative capability, of which he is a model practitioner. Wagenknecht avoids the easy condemnation and praise of Isabel's character that others indulge in as he argues that 'the ordeal (Isabel) undergoes is carefully prepared for' (p. 39). He reviews the plusses and minuses of each character in the novel (and provides a useful review of scholarship as he does), pointing out, for instance, that Osmond, traditionally seen as a heartless conspirator, was, as so reliable a witness as Ralph Touchett attests, very much in love with Isabel in the beginning.

Wagenknecht discounts Isabel's promise to Pansy as a reason for going back – either Pansy is as remarkable as her admirers think and will survive without anyone's aid or she is helpless and therefore Isabel's attempts at assistance will be futile; in fact, given Osmond's enmity toward Isabel, 'Pansy might well have to suffer more for Isabel's championship of her' (p. 50). A better reason might be that she has to immerse herself in the destructive element to save herself, to realize, by contrast, her own potential, and thus not end up like her aunt, Mrs Touchett, a shallow and unhappy woman. In keeping with his overall tone, Wagenknecht sees the novel's end as a bit of a Rorschach test: 'in the last analysis, what one believes about the ending of *The Portrait of a Lady* will be determined by what one believes about many other things' (pp. 51–2).

6   New criticism (theme)

It is not always easy to distinguish between New Critical studies that emphasize character and those that emphasize theme. In either case, of course, methodology is paramount: as opposed to a rhetoric-based impressionistic criticism that argues forcefully the critic's subjective reactions to the text, New Criticism of any kind attempts a cool, objective linking of the text's verifiable elements into a complex whole. Clearly, it is only by considering a given essay in the context of dozens of others like it that the student of criticism can feel comfortable in the act of classification.

Even then, 'pure' criticism of one school or another exists only in the literary handbooks and not in actual practice. For example, Seymour Kleinberg begins with a consideration of Isabel Archer's character (and not a favourable one, either) but then broadens his focus to include other characters and, ultimately, the theme of sexuality in *The Portrait of a Lady*. To Kleinberg, Isabel is a 'completely misguided heroine, a woman in search of a self', is 'only remote' and not at all 'intellectual', even though her friends think so (p. 3). The men are all unsatisfactory: Caspar Goodwood is brutal, Warburton effete, Ralph Touchett chaste and dying, Osmond misogynistic. Furthermore, eros and agape, or the erotic and the affectionate, are at war in this novel, whereas they are united in normal, healthy, adult sexuality. To Isabel, Goodwood represents eros, Ralph Touchett agape. She rejects both and chooses instead Osmond, who will not force Isabel to examine her own troubled nature because he is identical to her in his own confused sexuality. No wonder, therefore, that she returns to Osmond at the end – 'she must struggle with the impulses she has always denied, she must return to the only commitments, poor as they are, she has ever made' (p. 6). This is her fate – 'to change her nature is like asking Oedipus to have been polite at the crossroads' (p. 7). She ends at the 'moment of her life when youth and its aspirations are truly finished', when the irresistible world of fantasy which has propelled her all along is now quite resistible. She knows that her difficulties are of her own making and that she can only do what she has promised to do, even though her actions will probably be futile. 'More than any other heroine in the nineteenth century, and more than most in the twentieth', writes Kleinberg, 'Isabel Archer depicts the modern tragedy of suffering without redemption' (p. 7). And that is what makes the novel and the reader's reaction to it rich and complex.

Philip Sicker's contribution to the discussion of the love theme involves a detailed look at the long and complex evolution of the theme of romantic love in James's fiction and the conclusion, ultimately, that there is a vital relationship between love and the quest for identity in the novels. In *The Portrait of a Lady*, Isabel's problem is that her image of an ideal husband is extremely restrictive. She wants someone to free her of the false social role her wealth has forced on her, which means he must be poor, and she needs someone who will encourage her own growth, which means he must be refined; that is to say, she needs someone wholly unconventional. So when she hears of the reclusive Osmond, she becomes infatuated with his image before even meeting him. And she develops a false sense of herself that corresponds to this one of Osmond. She wants to live for Osmond and Pansy and be selfless.

But in place of her ideal, Osmond turns out to be vain and vicious – 'like Desdemona, Isabel fell in love with the imagined sufferings her husband had borne, but she finds herself married, not to Othello, but to Iago' (p. 62). Of course, Osmond is fooled, too. But whereas 'she fell in love with an ideal of otherness and longed to define her role *in relation* to her beloved, Osmond, who is capable only of self-love, sought to enlarge his identity by making an ideal of feminine beauty an expression of himself' (p. 63). But the reader need not think of Isabel as a victim only of Osmond's selfishness, says Sicker, since she victimizes herself through her own pride. And because she is prideful, she insists on bearing her unhappiness alone – for all their differences, Isabel Archer and Gilbert Osmond share a fear of letting their masks slip in public.

If most of the thematic studies of *The Portrait of a Lady* deal with love or with the related themes of love and identity, a second large group treats the theme of redemption. A representative essay is one by Lyall H. Powers which focuses on what he describes as a rebirth scene in the last part of the novel. In opposing Osmond by returning to Gardencourt, Isabel first passes through a kind of wasteland where a perpetual winter reigns. When she gets to Gardencourt, the point is made that this was her starting point in adult life; Isabel even uses the word 'sacred' to describe the Touchett estate. But she cannot return to her original innocence. Instead, hers will be 'that higher innocence, that superior goodness, which comes to the fallen who are saved. The pattern here is the familiar one of the paradox of the fortunate fall.... The result of her spiritual rebirth is seen in her determination to return and confront the evil of the world, to work at the redemption of that evil, to do in short whatever work the spiritually regenerate necessarily do here below' (p. 153). She is not going back to maintain her sterile marriage to Osmond, then, for she knows that marriage to be evil and loathsome. Besides, the pattern of development in the novel points to quite another ending. Redeemed herself, Isabel goes back to redeem Pansy so that history will not repeat itself.

The virtue of the New Criticism is that it unifies an unwieldy text. But psychology tells us that while we may want to impose order where it does not exist, disorder is often the natural state. Subsequent critical modes, often psychological, philosophical, or political in nature, offer free-wheeling views of literature and life that make the New Critics seem like the genteel ironists that, perhaps, they are.

7   Post-new criticism

There is, at the time of this writing, no single successor to the New Criticism that dominates teaching and writing as that school did in its heyday; the most accurate assessment would be that gender studies, New Historical readings, and other methodologies based in politics and economics have dominance in the academy over such philosophical schools as phenomenology and deconstruction. For that reason, much post-New Critical writing is concerned with definition, articulation of principles, and jockeying for position within the learned hierarchy. Thus some of the best recent books elaborate method at the expense of individual texts (or at least of *The Portrait of a Lady*). The matter is further complicated by the fact that the newer methodologies, especially those that, like deconstruction and reader-response, are predicated on a text's ultimate meaninglessness, sometimes tend to mingle and overlap in a single essay. When a central religion falters, competing and (eventually) cross-pollinating cults will try to take its place, and as the New Criticism wanes, critical

methods will invariably interbreed. In the interest of clarity, what
follows is an attempt to identify some of the prominent post-New
Critical schools and their contributions to our understanding of *The
Portrait of a Lady*.

Phenomenology and deconstruction are both philosophically-
based schools of criticism. Phenomenology is a method of inquiry
propounded largely by Edmund Husserl in which pure phenomena
are analysed and everything speculative is 'bracketed' or eliminated
from consideration. In *The Phenomenology of Henry James*, Paul B.
Armstrong follows Paul Ricoeur's suggestion that 'texts speak of
possible worlds and of possible ways of orienting oneself in those
worlds' (p. x). Examining 'the paradox of the servile will', Armstrong
notes that *The Portrait of a Lady* has a thesis (possibility), an antithesis
(limitation), and finally a synthesis of the two (the servile will).
Isabel thinks her possibilities are virtually limitless and relishes
giddily her sense of freedom and power, but when she tries to ground
her freedom in a meaningful situation and finds herself caught in a
trap she herself has helped make, she suffers guilt and despair.
Synthesis is achieved, however, when she is born again into freedom
as she willingly accepts her bonds. The reader leaves her just as she
begins in earnest her search for a meaningful freedom, a search that
will be difficult because establishing right relations between Self and
Other is always thus.

If phenomenological criticism seeks to bracket distractions and
identify the essential nature of a text, deconstruction goes in a rather
different direction. Deconstruction looks upon a text as a collection of
codes and conventions that can be read in an infinite number of ways
and that therefore has no central truth to it. Based in the assaults of
Nietzsche, Freud and Heidegger on the idea of textual authority,
deconstruction opens as many entries as possible into the text while
denying any final coherence.

Deborah Esch argues that *The Portrait of a Lady* is not a portrait, as
James himself said (in a letter to Grace Norton); that is, it is not a
static picture which reveals Isabel Archer's identity. Rather, it is a
study of Isabel as reader of others or misreader of them – certainly she
misreads Osmond, as she reveals during her meditation when she
says she took only a partial view of him for the whole when she agreed
to marry. And she does the same in the final chapter, even though
Goodwood begs her not to mistake part for the whole (his exact words
are, as quoted by Esch, 'You must save what you can of your life; you

mustn't lose it all simply because you've lost a part' [p. 150]). Thus her decision to go back is a mistake, and even though it may lead to 'a future that would be something other than the repetition of a past error', critics are wrong who say the book is to be read ethically or morally, that is, in terms of Isabel's going back to rescue Pansy. To the contrary, *The Portrait of a Lady* 'continues to yield [nothing but] the text out of which the "portrait" of its critical future must be rendered' (p. 153).

In recent years, many critics dissatisfied with the apolitical nature of deconstruction (no meaning means any meaning, which is good philosophy but bad politics) have taken up a Marxist-tinged New Historicism. Michael T. Gilmore describes *The Portrait of a Lady* as a novel in which people are constantly compared to objects, especially works of art, and appreciated as much for their economic as for their aesthetic worth. And James himself participates in this commodification by creating 'the portrait of a lady' and offering it for sale in the literary marketplace in order to establish his reputation as a major novelist and make enough money to relieve his financial concerns. In addition, the novel has a further economic aspect. Ownership of individual persons is the basis of social relations, and not merely when villains are concerned. While Osmond is conspicuous in this respect, others treat humans as expensive and beautiful objects: Pansy's suitor Ned Rosier, for example, and even Ralph Touchett, who, shortly after meeting Isabel Archer, thinks it is like receiving a Titian by mail to hang on the wall. (Even Mrs Touchett refers to Isabel as 'a yard of calico'.)

Though the Civil War had settled the question of overt ownership of human beings, the rise of monopoly capitalism made the buying and selling of labour power, of men and women, more prevalent; thinkers as diverse as Henry Thoreau and Karl Marx argued against the suppression of the individual under industrial capitalism. In his Prefaces to *The Portrait of a Lady* and also *The American*, which he wrote at approximately the same time, James allies himself with capitalism by depicting the writer as a businessman trafficking in the products he creates. James is the owner, then, of his characters, and speaks in the two Prefaces of the joy of 'possession'. Yet he also negates his self-presentation of the writer as capitalist; he is too much the partisan of Isabel and the enemy of all the collectors in the novel to be comfortable with his own image as owner and manipulator of others. The ambivalence shows in James's narration, where he is sometimes the omniscient creator of a fictitious world and sometimes a reporter happening upon 'real' events that exist independently of him. So the novel as a whole is 'at once a rejection and a corollary of a social order in which some persons are the tools or commodities of others' (p. 74). The Pansy sub-plot, in which her father considers her a piece of property and rails against Warburton for treating her like a suite of apartments, reinforces the theme of proprietorship, and certainly the novel's end shows that one cannot ever be delivered from the commodity world.

It has been noted that schools of criticism complicate the task of the taxonomist by mingling and overlapping. Another problem in critical taxonomy is that methodologies may exist in either 'strong' forms, in which standard terminology is used and recognizable authority figures are invoked, or 'weak' forms that make the same kinds of statements while avoiding jargon and references to the movement's demigods. Thus Elizabeth Allen takes up the essentials of Michael T. Gilmore's argument but makes no reference to their historical and economic background. Allen argues that *The Portrait of a Lady* is a study of proprietorship and manipulation with two halves: a theoretical half that ends with the death of Mr Touchett and Isabel's inheritance and a second half that overlaps the first in which practical schemes regarding Isabel's fate are set up around her. While Isabel and Ralph Touchett are building castles in the air, Osmond and Merle are quite businesslike in exerting their control over her. Their handling of the passive Pansy should have been a warning to Isabel, but it is several years before the lesson of Pansy beomes clear; in the meantime, Isabel thinks she is making a free choice.

After the time lapse in which James summarizes the first few years of the marriage, the reader is introduced to a new Isabel, one who no longer has potential but is an object of static value. She is in the frame of her portrait and has been 'collected' by the acquisitive Osmond, though she does not realize it even now. As for the ending (and here Allen does make an historical reference, albeit a general one), Isabel recognizes that a surrender to sexuality would mean a loss of self. 'Just as the nineteenth-century feminists often reacted against ideas of sexual freedom because they saw them as encroaching on their personal and intellectual autonomy by imposing their "sex" on them too strongly, so it is as a part of the same retention of self, of a self-perceived being, that Isabel rejects Caspar. She goes back to Europe, back to the field of experience, resistance and continuing life' (p. 97).

It is not difficult to see how the field of gender criticism relates to the New Historicism. Edward Wagenknecht (above) examined Isabel's character in terms of literary stereotypes but without the explicit political backdrop essential to gender studies, while that context is essential to Alfred Habegger's more recent essay on gender in *The Portrait of a Lady*.

Habegger's essay is refreshing in that he concentrates on Gilbert Osmond and not Isabel Archer. Habegger agrees with other critics that Isabel is a blend of the perfect Victorian lady and the independent American girl, but he sees Osmond as someone rather more unique. No one whom Isabel meets earlier is satisfactory; Caspar Goodwood's pushy American masculinity renders him unacceptable, and Lord Warburton is so inextricably involved with the English nobility, his radical views notwithstanding, that Isabel would be forced to live with him on his terms, not hers. Nor does she wish to masculinize herself and become a careerist in a largely male field like Henrietta Stackpole. So when Osmond comes along, she is swept away by the idea that she can marry a man with none of the usual outward signs of masculinity – a career, a place in the world – and still retain her freedom. What she misses is Osmond's own revelation of the true nature of his character, as, for instance, when he says the only men he envies are the Sultan of Turkey, the Czar, and the Pope ('all somewhat sinister figures in contemporary Protestant America', notes Habegger [p. 72]). So the most important agent in Isabel's doom is 'a displaced American with a secret and very American fantasy of absolute rule over others – a dream of kingship' (p. 73). Habegger finds the deeply anti-masculine character of *The Portrait of a Lady* a flaw, believing James was wrong to equate male sexuality with selfishness.

Part Two: Appraisal

8 The growth of melodrama

The child being the father of the man, according to Wordsworthian precept, James was destined to be a melodramatist from his days of earliest memory. In the autobiographical *A Small Boy and Others* (1913), the author speaks of the authority wielded over him by over-done theatrical productions of Dickens's *Nicholas Nickleby* and lesser-known plays with such revealing titles as *The Cataract of the Ganges* (by W. T. Moncrieff, 1823) and a P. T. Barnum sketch called *Jocko or the Brazilian Ape*. Later, when he had come to disdain such juvenalia, the mature. James nonetheless wished for the melodramatist's power to mesmerize (and his concomitant ability to make money). Indeed, his otherworldly, even sacerdotal image notwithstanding, James's career was, as much as any other writer's, a never-ending voyage between the poles of art and commerce. No doubt the tone and structure of his most characteristic work, such as *The Portrait of a Lady*, can be accounted for by the fact that he was working in a medium that 'offered unexplored possibilities for craftsmanship and formal perfection', as Peter Brooks notes, 'yet remained rooted in the desire for compelling, exciting fabulation' (p. x).

How anomalous it is, though, to think of James, or at least the mature James, as a writer of melodrama. Without a doubt, he began as one; Brooks quotes his friend Thomas Sergeant Perry as saying that in James's lurid early writings, 'the heroes were for the most part villains, but they were white lambs by the side of the sophisticated heroines, who seemed to have read all Balzac in the cradle and to be positively dripping with lurid crimes. He began with these extravagant pictures of course in adoration of the great master whom he always so warmly admired' (p. 153). Guided by the dark strain in his own thought, a strain reinforced by the 'lurid' and 'extravagant' images and themes not only of Balzac but also his American master Hawthorne, James produced such Gothic-tinged romances as *Watch and Ward* (1878) and *Roderick Hudson*, the heavily-Gothic *The American* and *The Turn of the Screw*, as well as the covert melodramas of *The Portrait of a Lady* and *The Wings of the Dove* (1902).

For all that, 'melodrama' is a tawdry term to most readers, especially in regard to the work of a writer's writer like James. Certainly he himself uses the word in his critical writings as a term of opprobrium, having as it does the connotations (according to Brooks) of 'indulgence of strong emotionalism; moral polarization and schematization; extreme states of being, situations, actions; overt villainy, persecution of the good, and final reward of virtue; inflated and extravagant expression; dark plottings, suspense, breathtaking peripety' (pp. 11–12). As much as James denigrates melodrama, though, he also reveals it to be one of his guilty pleasures, at least in retrospect, and in his notebooks – that is, in the personal journals, not the public critical essays – he invokes Scribe, Sardou and the other masters of the well-made French theatrical melodrama when he expresses his longing to be a more popular author.

Besides, once one puts aside the images of howling heroines and moustache-twisting villains (today derived largely from the lithographed advertisements for the plays which may or may not depict with accuracy what actually occurred on stage), one realizes how many of the characteristics of the melodrama enumerated by Brooks are either present in or just beneath the surface of *The Portrait of a Lady*. Moreover, the moral and epistemological ground of the novel is the same as that of the genre as a whole. Throughout, reader, novelist, narrator, secondary characters and Isabel Archer too seem to be asking if, in a changing world, Isabel is doing the best thing for herself and if the others are doing their best for her.

As Brooks says, melodrama 'comes into being in a world where the traditional imperatives of truth and ethics have been violently thrown into question, yet where the promulgation of truth and ethics, their instauration as a way of life, is of immediate, daily, political concern'. The word 'political' may seem out of place in a discussion of *The Portrait of a Lady*, but not if one appreciates, as did Ezra Pound, the James who argued for individual freedom and against the tyranny of oppression in virtually all his novels. Brooks continues: 'Melodrama from its inception takes as its concern ... the location, expression, and imposition of basic ethical and psychic truths. It says them over and over in clear language, it rehearses their conflicts and combats, it reenacts the menace of evil and the eventual triumph of morality made operative and evident'. While the novel does not so much re-state basic truths as it does re-dramatize them for characters who have forgotten or been blinded to them, *The Portrait of a Lady* is, like all of James's writing, not ideological but expressive; it seeks, not to give voice to ideas, but (as critics of James who find him long-winded will doubtless agree) to give voice. Or as Brooks says, 'While [melodrama's] social implications may be variously revolutionary or conservative, it is in all cases radically democratic, striving to make its representations clear and legible to everyone' (p. 15). If one of those to whom James is striving to make things clear is himself, then we have another reason for the density and complexity of a prose in which the basic elements of melodrama are, when they are not actually on the surface of his writing, at least never very far from it.

As the reader has seen in the section on source criticism, James's tendency is to both replicate the essence of any source material as well as establish arguments against it; often it is that core of tradition as well as James's critical examination of it that accounts for the richness of his narrative. Brooks is not the only critic to have noticed the melodramatic basis of James's fictional world and also James's quarrel with the genre; Leo Levy observes that while the figure of Osmond reveals 'most clearly the didactic basis of [*The Portrait of a Lady's*] melodrama' and that he is 'a figure of unrelieved malignancy, but scarcely a believable human being', James is torn between the two modes of representation he uses in such earlier novels as *Washington Square* (1880), in which he wants clearly to excoriate the victim yet is aware of the factors that make him what he is (p. 46). When Isabel realizes she has married a monster, she acts in a manner many readers regard as unrealistic or at least unsatisfactory, yet that is not only what James wants but also what the genre requires – 'a widened, irreparable breach, marked by calculated opportunism turned to scorn and hatred on one side, and a long-suffering, enduring virtue on the other.' This, says Levy, 'is melodrama, for it is the display of a morality that abandons awareness of the involutions in which good and evil entwine themselves in order to state more dramatically their necessary conflict' (p. 48). When Isabel returns to Osmond, even readers who approve the action ultimately are dismayed, since Isabel's many good qualities suggest that she deserves a better fate. Yet the return 'deepens these contrasts to the blackened shades of melodrama by asserting that the coexistence of absolute evil with an harassed and defensive good is the distinctive feature of moral experience' (p. 51).

This is all very well for the literary historian in general and the student of melodrama in particular, but readers often want more closure than is found in a novel like *The Portrait of a Lady* – if not outright triumph on the part of a deserving heroine, at least an end to her misery. The matter would be easier to resolve were James a novelist pure and simple, but the quantity and complexity of his work, the breadth of epistemological and moral concern (what do we know? what do we do about it?) explain why more than one Jacobite, from the young writers who called him 'the Master' in his own lifetime to present-day readers, consider James a teacher as well.

Like other great teachers, James appears in a time of crisis. He lived in a parlous time, a period in which the social and moral fabric began to fray and then, with the outbreak of the First World War, to unravel entirely. His fictions are both attempts to preserve the best of that era and to examine it critically as it disappears; more important, his fictions are vindications of the individual's right to perceive and misperceive, to see and be blind to the implications of his or her actions, to understand and fail to understand, to accept responsibility for his or her vision, however cloudy it may be. Outside of a shared value system which no longer existed, his characters' best efforts were to express all, to articulate everything.

A garrulous genre like melodrama is, in one sense, perfect for the nineteenth century. It is no accident that the success of melodramatic fiction is linked to the rise of the middle class. As the middle class grew in size and prosperity, so too did its members' partly guilty, partly disdainful curiosity about the class they were leaving as well as their anticipatory curiosity about the one they hoped to join. Consequently, the novel prospered as it fulfilled its traditional role of serving as an inexpensive source of 'information' about the poor and the rich. A failure-proof recipe for successful fiction calls for the author to (1) describe the lives of the rich or the poor for the middle-class reader and (2) reinforce that reader's notion of his or her superiority to these others. A mass of detail, a dash of morality, and an author is on his way to best-sellerdom.

The difference is that James gives the detail in abundance but withholds the comforting morality. It is a reader's commonplace that

James is an 'ambiguous' writer, but 'ambiguous' has two connotations. It may mean 'doubtful or uncertain', but it may also mean
'susceptible of more than one interpretation'. This second definition
is the one that applies to James's writing. And in this second sense of
the term, it is precisely the ambiguity of James's writing that makes
him relatively easy to read, despite some readers' assertions. He is
easy to read because he is not 'about' anything, and therefore the
reader need have no preconceptions. James is a master teacher not
because he is didactic but because he is painstaking and as clear-
sighted as one can be in his unclear world. Hence the attraction of the
most expressive, the most garrulous of genres.

9 A post-revolutionary genre

Peter Brooks explains that as a genre melodrama was born in the
context of the French Revolution and its aftermath and that it seeks
new definitions in a world without fixed values. Tragedy, a pre-
Revolutionary genre, seeks resolutions for moral problems that are
easily apprehended within the framework of a shared value system.
In contrast, melodrama can only attempt to express all, to articulate
everything. Brooks says that 'the ritual of melodrama involves the
confrontation of clearly identified antagonists and the expulsion of
one of them', even though 'it can offer no terminal reconciliation, for
there is no longer a clear transcendent value' (p. 17). Clearly this is
the case in *The Portrait of a Lady* (as it will be also in *The Turn of the
Screw*). The wronged Isabel Archer is in the right, regardless of her
complicity in her downfall, and the neutral-seeming or even desirable
Osmond is identified as a villain before the novel is done, then expel-
led from his role of benign husband and *pater familias*. And of course
there is no reconciliation, no embrace of transcendent values, as the
abundance of criticism makes clear.

   Post-Revolutionary though it is, melodrama does not refute pre-
Revolutionary values. On the contrary, it tries to re-establish these
values and then admits the impossibility of doing so. As Brooks notes,
'melodrama represents both the urge toward resacralization and the
impossibility of conceiving sacralization other than in personal
terms' (p. 16). Thus melodramatic heroines like Isabel are described
so that the reader thinks of them as pure, saintly, nun-like, angelic
and so on (cf. Isabel's equally-wronged literary ancestor, that New

England nun Hester Prynne). Even their sins are the sins of saints –
Osmond and Merle are adulterous and deceptive, but Isabel is
merely proud. And if melodrama looks back almost wistfully to pre-
cepts of theism, it also looks forward to a post-theistic world in which
both damnation and salvation are personal in nature. To Brooks,
'the Gothic castle, with its pinnacles and dungeons, crennallations,
moats, drawbridges, spiraling staircases and concealed doors, realizes an architectural approximation of the Freudian model of the
mind, particularly the traps laid for the conscious by the unconscious
and the repressed'. In America particularly, those clear-thinking
masters of reason (Jefferson, Franklin, the Adamses) who founded
a system based on the thought of European rationalists (Locke,
Rousseau, Voltaire) described a sun-drenched, harmonious world
that was beautiful yet incomplete. Just as these philosophical and
political thinkers fought against unreason, so in their way did the
romancers and melodramatists fight for it. Or as Brooks notes, 'the
Gothic novel seeks an epistemology of the depths; it is fascinated by
what lies hidden in the dungeon and the sepulcher' (p. 19).

Is James not thus fascinated, both with the subtler workings of the
mind as well as with the palpable horrors of Gothic settings, as seen in
Osmond's various yet equally evil abodes? Is not the chapter that
James himself most admired and to which most critics give signal
attention a representation of profound introspection within a deeply
expressionistic *mise-en-scène*, an overlay, as it were, of mental and
Gothic architecture? Brooks says that the melodramatist is preoc-
cupied 'with nightmare states, with claustration and thwarted
escape, with innocence buried alive and unable to voice its claim to
recognition' (p. 20). To realize how much a melodramatist James is,
one need think only of the cloistered Claire de Cintré in *The American*,
Pansy and Isabel in this novel, the governess in *The Turn of the Screw*,
and the less-physically stifled heroes and heroines of the later novels
(Hyacinth Robinson of *The Princess Casamassima* (1886), Maisie of
What Maisie Knew (1897), Milly Theale of *The Wings of the Dove*) who
are no less surely deceived and betrayed than the more traditionally
melodramatic characters.

To this point, the terms 'Gothic novel' and 'melodrama' have been
used virtually interchangeably. While it is true that the two share
many characteristics, it should be observed that melodrama has a
greater ethical dimension than does Gothicism. In the Gothic novel,
ghosts, portentous omens and calamitous events occur more for their

own sake than as an assertion of moral evil; the heroine owes her exalted stature more to the fact that she is being menaced than to any innate or empirically-developed superiority. But because melodrama is asserting itself in an age of no fixed values, it allays the reader's fears by permitting both monstrous, deliberate evil and an equally urgent (and eventually triumphant) virtue; as Brooks says, melodrama 'diverges from the Gothic novel in its optimism, its claim that the moral imagination can open up the angelic spheres as well as the demonic depths and can allay the threat of moral chaos' (p. 20). Melodrama is not moralistic, of course, but expressionistic. Melodrama in general and a novel like *The Portrait of a Lady* in particular dramatize morality and promote, not an ideology, but the virtue of the moral struggle for its own sake.

As a literary genre, melodrama runs parallel to what Brooks identifies as the enduring systems of 'expressionistic clarification' in Western culture, those of Marx, Hegel and Freud. Of these, psychoanalysis has particular application to a consideration of melodrama. In both, hierarchies of conflicting entities, be they ego, id and superego or hero, villain and confidant, wage unremitting and potentially disabling war on each other; in both, the strenuous workings of the process itself is more significant than any received ethical framework. Moreover, 'psychoanalysis as the "talking cure" further reveals its affinity with melodrama, the drama of articulation' (pp. 203–4).

Just as it would be wrong to equate melodrama with Gothicism at its point of origin, so too would it be a mistake to equate this garrulous genre with the more contemporary school of deconstructive writing. Deconstruction denies an end; melodrama pushes toward one, as does psychoanalysis. Of course, melodrama and psychoanalysis may never reach the promised closure; cures are notoriously hard to come by on the psychoanalyst's couch, and it may be that the weekly meetings themselves are the cure. Doubtless the analytical sessions would be ineffectual did not the analysand believe that a finite end obtainable, just as Isabel Archer seems unlikely to make a difference in her world unless she believes that she can. By remaining open-ended, *The Portrait of a Lady* underscores James's belief in the process of teaching, acting and articulating for its own sake. Too, the book thus places itself within the tradition of Hugo, Balzac, Dickens, Dostoevsky, Conrad, Lawrence and Faulkner, says Peter Brooks, but not that of Flaubert, Maupassant, Beckett, Robbe-Grillet, Joyce and Kafka. The writers of the Flaubertian counter-tradition 'set against the ambitions of melodramatism an attitude of deconstructive and stoic materialism, and a language of deflationary suspicion.' In contrast, those of the Balzacian school (including James) 'remain convinced that the surface of the world – the surfaces of manners, the signifiers of the text – are indices pointing to hidden forces and truths, latent signifieds. . . . The gestures recorded in the text must be metaphoric of something else.'

As Isabel's exhausting quest suggests, 'the direct articulation of central meanings is difficult, dangerous, and even impossible. But this is not viewed as reason to abandon the search for them' (pp. 198–9). Outside the Third World, the good news about modern life is that most peoples do not have to live under a single, absolute authority. The bad news is that there are despots everywhere, within and without, and that many of them are as attractive initially as Osmond is to Isabel. Our confidants, our teachers, analysts and melodramatists are there to help us, but ultimately we must save ourselves. In doing so, we may find that salvation lies in the pursuit of freedom and not in the obtaining of it.

10   Starting from loneliness

Thus far, the emphasis has been on the professional rationale for James's role as melodramatist. Before the text proper is examined, it would be appropriate to say a word about the author's personal affinity for that role. More than any writer of the past hundred years, James represents the Great Solitary, the high priest of art whose devotion is a curious mixture of self-indulgence and sacrifice. James chose deliberately to have no wife, no lovers, no children, no career. Like all writers, he wrote out of himself, but since he had comparatively little life outside of his art, and since his fiction is hardly self-reflexive (with the exception of a handful of short stories such as 'The Figure in the Carpet' [1896] and 'The Lesson of the Master' [1888]), he must have been writing out of something deeper than either life or art. In one sense, one may say that loneliness is the well out of which James's fiction flowed. The novelist Desmond McCarthy recorded an anecdote (quoted by Gordon Pirie) that speaks volumes on this subject.

> It occurred after a luncheon party of which he had been, as they say, 'the life'. We happened to be drinking our coffee together while

the rest of the party had moved on to the verandah. 'What a charming picture they make', he said, with his great head aslant, 'the women with their embroidery, the ...' There was nothing in his words, anybody might have spoken them; but in his attitude, in his voice, in his whole being at that moment, I divined such complete detachment, that I was startled into speaking out of myself: 'I can't bear to look at life like that,' I blurted out, 'I want to be in everything. Perhaps that is why I cannot *write*, it makes me feel absolutely alone ...' The effect of this confession upon him was instantaneous and surprising. He leant forward and grasped my hand excitedly: 'Yes, it is solitude. If it runs after you and catches you, well and good. But for heaven's sake don't run after *it*. It is absolute solitude'. And he got up hurriedly and joined the others. (p. 31)

Loneliness both punishes and rewards, then. And so does community: James's letters and notebooks make clear how devoted he was to his friends and family, yet these same writings reveal the need for solitude as a prerequisite for the writer's life.

If loneliness is the great enemy in James's fiction, then each liaison is a *liaison dangereuse*. Daisy Miller in the story by that name (1878), Christopher Newman and Claire de Cintré in *The American*, Isabel Archer, Hyacinth Robinson in *The Princess Casamassima*, Milly Theale in *The Wings of the Dove*, and a host of other characters want desperately to love, yet love humiliates, crushes, and, in some cases, destroys them. In *The Spoils of Poynton*, when Fleda Vetch realizes that Owen Gereth does actually love her, the epiphany is expressed in a burst of joyful lyricism, yet 'the strangest thing of all was the momentary sense of desolation' (p. 161). And as we shall see below, as Isabel Archer listens to the declaration of love she has so wanted from Osmond, she feels as though she hears a bolt sliding and wonders whether she is being locked up. No wonder James seems to be 'working it out' constantly, writing his way toward the best possible solution in a world without shared values.

Perhaps the orphaned Hyacinth Robinson is the character who illustrates most melodramatically the strenuousness of the choices we all must make yet which no one seems to be able to make satisfactorily. Forced to choose between a morally upright but impoverished loneliness and friendship with those who would enrich yet manipulate him, Hyacinth chooses the one solution that puts a period to the flow of words: he kills himself, and the novel ends. Before he does so, though, Hyacinth is described as the quintessential Jamesian 'passionate observer' in an image the author found so apt that he used it again in two other works. This image, which occurs also in *What Maisie Knew* and in James's autobiography, is of a child with his face flattened against the window of a candy store, fascinated with the sweetmeats he will never eat but which he possesses passionately with his eyes and mind. That James described his young self this way as well as two of his fictional children suggests both the fundamental reality of this paradoxical stance and the continuing importance of it to him in his mature years.

This is how we meet James, this is how we leave him: not removed from life, not in it, but passionately desirous of life and, at the same time, separated from it by the sheerest of barriers. The image never changed from its first occurrence to its last; the child never enters the candy store, never leaves the window. All that is left is the 'talking cure' of art.

11   The prisoner

With the triumphs of *Roderick Hudson*, 'Daisy Miller', and *The American* behind him, James was ready to write a new kind of novel. *The Portrait of a Lady* advances considerably the notion of realism represented by the Jane Austen-George Eliot school; to do this, James had to invent a hardier pioneer than had ever inhabited his fiction before. We can appreciate how much greater a vessel of consciousness than any previous Jamesian character his new heroine is if we compare the reactions of the good-hearted but limited Christopher Newman to Europe and those of Isabel Archer. When she visits Saint Peter's Cathedral in Rome, the narrator notes that 'her conception of greatness rose and rose' and 'after this it never lacked space to soar' (p. 343). Everything she sees is new, even if she has already seen it; she visits the gallery of the Capitol with others to view the statuary, but when she re-visits it alone, even though 'she had seen them all before ... her enjoyment repeated itself, and it was all the greater because she was glad again, for the time, to be alone' (p. 354). This may be contrasted with Newman's dutiful visits to the great artworks of Europe and his complete willingness to adopt the attitudes toward them suggested by his Baedeker guide. Touring Greece, Turkey and Egypt with Madame Merle, 'Isabel travelled rapidly and recklessly;

she was like a thirsty person draining cup after cup' (p. 374). And whereas Newman cheerfully forgets all the art he has seen, 'Isabel ... made use of her memory of Rome as she might have done, in a hot and crowded room, of a phial of something pungent hidden in her hand-kerchief' (p. 371).

What James appears to have done is to create an infinitely capacious character in order to treat a limitless theme. The earlier novels contain signal instances of self-dramatization: in *Roderick Hudson*, Roderick and Rowland Mallet represent the committed and the cautious attitudes toward life and art that the young Henry James struggled with, and Christopher Newman of *The American* shares James's sense of frustration at being unable to penetrate a closed Parisian society. In order to write a novel about freedom and its limitations, James not only had to feel his theme but to dramatize it, as he makes clear in those revealing passages from the novel's preface where he elaborates on his identification with his heroine. There he speaks of 'the fascinations of the fabulist's art, these lurking forces of expansion, these necessities of upspringing in the seed, these beautiful determinations, on the part of the idea entertained, to grow as tall as possible, to push into the light and air and thickly flower there' (p. 43). For 'the idea entertained' to 'grow as tall as possible', James resolves on a new method of writing: '"Place the center of the subject in the young woman's own consciousness", I said to myself, "and you get as interesting and as beautiful a difficulty as you could wish"' (p. 50).

But freedom, 'the idea entertained', is apparent only against the contrasting background of restraint; that is what makes it interesting and beautiful yet difficult. The novel begins late in the afternoon, the time of day, according to Adeline Tintner, that is associated with the high, sweet, melancholy tone of the Arcadian tradition (not the buoyant pastoral mode, whose time of day is noon). The narrator revels in the late-life freedom of old Daniel Touchett, whose unusually large, brilliantly-painted tea cup suggests his openness to the good life, as does his reconstruction outside of a lavish sitting room complete with carpets, cushioned seats, books and papers. When Isabel is introduced into this scene in all the fullness of her promise, a question is imposed implicitly: is all this freedom, this openness, available to someone like her? That is the great question of this and perhaps any melodrama. It is also one that will not be answered as such questions usually are in more traditional fiction;

instead, the question of Isabel's freedom will be refined into more specific questions. When Ralph Touchett hears that his cousin is 'quite independent', he asks, 'But who's "quite independent", and in what sense is the term used? ... Does the term apply more particularly to the young lady my mother has adopted, or does it characterize her sisters equally? – and is it used in a moral or in a financial sense? Does it mean that they've been left well off, or that they wish to be under no obligations? or does it simply mean that they're fond of their own way?' (p. 67). In posing these questions, clearly Ralph is speaking not merely for himself; Isabel, the other characters, the narrator and the reader will consider these questions as well before the melodrama is played out.

The eligible male characters in the novel seem not only narrow but also bent on greater narrowness; they wish to marry and settle down, to limit themselves and the women they profess to love. In addition to being constrained by the desire to marry, each has a further limitation: Warburton is hobbled by his responsibilities, Touchett by illness, and Goodwood (the most promising) by his enslaving ardour. Throughout his writings and particularly in the preface and first chapter of *The Portrait of a Lady*, James makes it clear that only a woman can be really free.

Of course, her love of freedom leads Isabel to choose Gilbert Osmond, in part because he does not seem to have the limitations of her other suitors. The novel is predicated on Isabel's making this mistake, discovering that she has made it, and learning the lesson of her folly. Borrowing a central image from the Gothic tradition, James will make Isabel into a prisoner, not only immuring her in prison-like structures but also showing how she has trapped herself in the labyrinth of her own rigid thinking. Completing the humbling process in which Copernicus revealed that the earth is not the centre of the universe and Darwin showed that human destiny is biologically and not divinely determined, Freud demonstrated – and a character like Isabel Archer proves – that an individual is not even the mistress of her own house.

But it is not as though she goes from freedom to imprisonment as the novel progresses; from the beginning, she evidences what Daniel Schneider (above) calls 'the divided self'. When her aunt discovers her in Albany, she finds an Isabel who has more or less locked herself away in the musty old office of the family home, where she reads and dreams of the outside world. An unmarried woman with few social connections, Isabel is a prisoner of circumstance, yet 'her imagination was by habit ridiculously active; when the door was not open it jumped out the window' (p. 86). After Mrs Touchett takes her up, Isabel acquires an extraordinary amount of freedom, but she retains a nostalgia for her cell, as it were, saying to Ralph Touchett on meeting the nun-like Misses Molyneux (Warburton's sisters), '"I think it's lovely to be so quiet and reasonable and satisfied"' (p. 130). And this at the very start of her social and matrimonial adventures.

At first glance, it would seem that Isabel could hardly do better than Warburton. Gentle and devoted, he is also a man of his times, a perfect representative of the aristocrat in the post-Revolutionary world. Ralph Touchett explains that he has 'great responsibilities, great opportunities, great consideration, great wealth, great power, a natural share in the public affairs of a great country. But he's all in a muddle about himself, his position, his power, and indeed about everything in the world. He's the victim of a critical age; he has ceased to believe in himself and he doesn't know what to believe in' (p. 125) He is not only an ideal hero for the melodrama but also an ideal candidate for Isabel's hand, since she has no interest in being forced into someone else's mould. Warburton's freethinking notwithstanding, Isabel feels that 'a territorial, a political, a social magnate had conceived the design of drawing her into the system in which he rather invidiously lived and moved' (p. 156). When Warburton proposes, James describes Isabel's reaction with an apt image: 'though she was lost in admiration of her opportunity she managed to move back into the deepest shade of it, even as some wild, caught creature in a vast cage' (p. 162). Horrified of limitations yet desirous of quiet and retreat, Isabel reacts in a manner that conveys her self-division. If the image of the cowering, caged animal suggests entrapment, it suggests shelter as well.

The scenes in which Isabel rebuffs Caspar Goodwood are remarkably similar to the ones in which she struggles against the restrictive security Warburton offers, with the added difference that the passionate Goodwood represents a more physically unsettling threat – as well as, of course, a more physically appealing attractiveness. Like Warburton, Goodwood disputes Isabel's claim that he will restrict her: 'He had never supposed she hadn't wings and the need of beautiful free movements. ... "Who would wish less to curtail your liberty than I? What can give me greater pleasure than to see you perfectly independent – doing whatever you like? It's to make you

independent that I want to marry you" ("That's a beautiful
sophism"', Isabel replies [p. 214]). The image of the caged bird joins
that of the prisoner, the cloistered nun, and the trapped beast in
suggesting how apparent Isabel's love of freedom is to the other
characters. For her would-be 'liberators' (her aunt, Warburton, Caspar Goodwood) to mention it so frequently is to indicate their awareness of freedom's fragility in an enslaving world. In Goodwood's case,
he seems to protest too much. As Isabel thinks that 'the idea of a
diminished liberty was particularly disagreeable to her at present,
since she had just given a sort of personal accent to her independence
by looking so straight at Lord Warburton's big bribe and yet turning
away from it', she cannot help being aware that Goodwood 'insisted,
ever, with his whole weight and force' (p. 169). Apparently Goodwood has the misfortune not merely to be a potential jailer but also to
look like one.

Throughout the novel, the abstract ideal of freedom is treated as
laudable, but the actual practice of freedom is always being called
into question; Goodwood is not the only one to warn Isabel that an
unmarried woman, despite her surface independence, is restricted in
many ways. Besides, the reader must remember that part of Isabel
doesn't want to be free. Shortly after refusing Goodwood, she thinks
to herself that she wants only to 'case herself again in brown holland'
(that is, the cloth used to cover furniture in an owner's absence) and
be 'still', a word that recalls the nun-like 'quiet' she associates with
the Misses Molyneux (p. 217). Two pages later, in one of the novel's
most celebrated images, Isabel tells Henrietta Stackpole, who has
asked her if she knows where she is drifting, ' "No, I haven't the least
idea, and I find it very pleasant not to know. A swift carriage, of a dark
night, rattling with four horses over roads that one can't see – that's
my idea of happiness"'. The melodrama of the novel's first half
is subsumed in this open-ended image of a character who, like
Flaubert's Emma Bovary ('the heroine of an immoral novel', says the
cynical Stackpole), proclaims that she will free herself through
adventure when actually she is submitting to the control of exterior
forces and, as Henrietta Stackpole says, ' "drifting to some great mistake"' (p. 219).

As soon as the seeming freedom of Mr Touchett's money is con-
ferred on Isabel, enter Gilbert Osmond, who throws into question the
liberating power of money by suggesting how great a lure it is to such
a jailer as himself. Significantly, we see his house before we see him,

and just as the Touchett estate prepares the reader pictorially for the freedom and openness of the first half of the book, so Osmond's Florentine villa represents the imprisonment that will occur in the second. Its 'imposing front had a somewhat incommunicative character. It was the mask, not the face of the house. It had heavy lids, but no eyes.... The windows of the ground floor ... seemed less to offer communication with the world than to defy the world to look in. They were massively cross-barred, and placed at such a height that curiosity, even on tiptoe, expired before it could reach them' (pp. 278–9). The actual villa on which Osmond's is based and where James himself lived for a time is located outside Florence on the hill of Bellosguardo. The face of the Villa Castellani (its name has since been changed to the Villa Mercede) is indeed an eyeless mask, with heavily stuccoed and cross-barred windows. Later, when Isabel enters the villa, she gets a distinct sense of there being 'something grave and strong in the place; it looked somehow as if, once you were in, you would need an act of energy to get out' (p. 304). Of course, this is only one of several such hints about Osmond's character that Isabel chooses to ignore.

And just as the villa looks like a prison, so its chief occupant acts very much like a jailer. In his first appearance, Gilbert Osmond is seen giving orders to his compliant daughter Pansy regarding her convent education; in this he is aided by nuns who, like Madame Merle, seem almost eager to betray their sex. Osmond's oppressiveness is subtle, as befits the villain of a melodrama that is more or less covert. Indeed, his life-long vow 'to be as quiet as possible' is one of his strongest appeals to the like-minded Isabel (p. 315). But if he is clever at concealing his true nature from Isabel, he has no need to be so deceptive to his co-conspirator, Madame Merle, to whom he says that Isabel's only fault is she has 'too many ideas' (p. 335). Within a few pages of first meeting Osmond, the reader intuits that he intends to imprison Isabel not only physically but mentally and spiritually as well.

Would that Isabel, an avid reader, were aware of all the sinister Osmonds in the writings of Monk Lewis and other Gothicists! In his brilliant and exhaustive study of connections between *The Portrait of a Lady* and popular literature, William Veeder details Osmond's evil literary pedigree, only a portion of which is reported here:

Seeking a name for his villain in *The Castle Spectre*, Monk Lewis may well have gone back (consciously or unconsciously) to a bloody and exotic drama of the British theatrical past, *Osmond, the Great Turk*. For certain we find in Lewis' perenially popular play several details so similar to details in *The Portrait* that we should examine them. *The Castle Spectre* contains, for example, a 'knave' named Gilbert (I i). His master is 'Osmond ... the very antidote of mirth' (I i). In his pursuit of the heroine, Osmond is thwarted by 'the Portrait of a Lady' (III iii) which swings back to reveal a convenient passage-way and by the lady of that portrait, who comes back (as a ghost) to save her daughter from incarceration by Osmond. Before the Beset Heroine escapes, however, she endures a dark night 'allowed you to reflect upon your situation' (III iii). (I cannot resist adding that the heroine's duenna exclaims, 'oh gemini' [III iii].) After *The Castle Spectre* we find the romantics christening characters 'Osman' and 'Osmyn' and the name 'Ormond' appearing in both Maria Edgeworth and Charles Brockden Brown. In America the name Osmond itself appears as early as 1804, in Alicia La Fanu's *Lucy Osmond*. This story of betrayed heroines, inadequate guardians, and sudden fortunes is then followed in the 1830s by a terrifically successful play, *Lucy Leslie, the Cottager's Daughter; or, the Maid, the Mother and the Maniac*. Here poor Lucy is shot down by her betrayer, Osmond, when he learns she is not, as he has been led to believe, the heiress to fifty thousand pounds'. (pp. 120–1)

Isabel is, if prideful, never stupid, and if she loves Osmond, nonetheless some part of her is aware of the menace he represents; when Osmond first professes his love for her, 'the tears came into her eyes: this time they obeyed the sharpness of the pang that suggested to her somehow the slipping of a fine bolt – backward, forward, she couldn't have said which' (p. 360). Her cousin Ralph, clearly the best example of the Jamesian 'passionate observer' in the novel, knows that Osmond means to restrict Isabel's freedom. He warns her: '"You seemed to me to be soaring far up in the blue – to be sailing in the bright light, over the heads of men. Suddenly some one tosses up a faded rosebud – a missile that should never have reached you – and straight you drop to the ground"'. When Isabel fails to respond to Ralph's metaphor, he describes Osmond's imprisoning instincts more explicitly, calling him 'small', 'narrow', 'selfish' (pp. 395–6).

When, after several years of marriage, Isabel remarks that Osmond has '"a genius for upholstery"', she seems cognizant of the fact that he is, as Ralph described him, 'a sterile dilettante' (pp. 436, 396). But even before then, she strikes the reader as aware, at least on a subliminal level, that Osmond is a collector of people as well as art objects. If the image of Osmond as the warden of enormous, prison-like structures is almost too Gothic to be believable, it is offset by an opposite kind of image: of him as the curator of a cabinet of bibelots. At first, Isabel is flattered that Osmond has selected her. After Osmond has declared himself but before they are married, Isabel thinks to herself that she 'felt older – ever so much, and as if she were "worth more" for it, like some curious piece in an antiquary's collection' (p. 377). What makes this innocent, even self-complimentary comparison sinister is the amplification of it several pages later, this time from Osmond's viewpoint. He reflects that 'Madame Merle had made him a present of incalculable value' and even specifies his 'curious piece' as 'a silver plate' with 'a polished, elegant surface' that will reflect his thoughts, 'a plate that he might heap up with ripe fruits, to which it would give a decorative value, so that talk might become for him a sort of served dessert'. Osmond's cold sadism lurks beneath the surface and is never expressed physically, but it always seems about to, as when he thinks that 'he could tap her imagination with his knuckle and make it ring' (p. 401).

The negative association of women with art objects is rife in the second half of the novel, as, for instance, when Merle says to Osmond, who is examining one of her bibelots, ' "I've seen better what you have been to your wife than I ever saw what you were for me. Please be very careful of that precious object" ', and he responds to her double *entendre* with a yonic equation of his own: ' "It already has a wee bit of a tiny crack", said Osmond dryly as he put it down' (p. 570). The putdowns continue; the objectification of women carries over into the conversations between Osmond and Ned Rosier about the latter's desire to marry Pansy, and once again the sexually-suggestive word 'piece' is used; Rosier asks if Osmond is ' "not thinking of parting with a – a piece or two?" ', and later Osmond tells him, ' "I set a great price on my daughter" ' (pp. 418, 429). In another conversation about another suitor, Osmond continues to discuss his daughter as though she were property. After Warburton has expressed a passing interest in Pansy (more as a means for maintaining his proximity to Isabel than for any other reason) and then moved on, Osmond complains to Isabel that Warburton has treated Pansy as one might treat a suite of apartments, trying it out gratis for a while and then deciding not to take it.

'"And he goes away after having got a month's lodging in the poor little apartment for nothing"', says Osmond, his language betraying him once more (p. 538). The cumulative effect of his unflattering references to wife and daughter is to make him sound not merely like a jailer but also a seller of slaves, even a pimp.

Osmond is so much the icy curator that he seems to use the language of curatorship unconsciously, as when he tells Isabel, '"You're certainly not fortunate in your intimates; I wish you might make a new collection"' (p. 537). For all the aesthetic veneer, though, he reveals the ferocity of his intent rarely yet unforgettably. The gentility of the Jamesian world is so uniform that departures from it are doubly memorable, and so it is when Osmond, on learning that Rosier has declared his feelings for Pansy, announces that 'he ought to be horsewhipped' (p. 425). Rosier has a surprisingly well-developed sense of Osmond's viciousness and is able to intuit what it takes Isabel years to discover, perhaps because he possesses at least some of the collecting instinct that Osmond has in abundance. For example, Rosier thinks of Osmond's sinisterly-named Palazzo Roccanera ('black rock') as 'a palace by Roman measure, but a dungeon to poor Rosier's apprehensive mind. It seemed to him of evil omen that the young lady he wished to marry . . . should be immured in a kind of domestic fortress, a pile which bore a stern old Roman name, which smelt of historic deeds, of crime and craft and violence. . . .'

In James's New England imagination, the connection between the dark practices of the Church of Rome and those of more literal prisons that is detailed so harrowingly in *The American* is made again; the narrator relates that 'Rosier was haunted by the conviction that at picturesque periods young girls had been shut up there to keep them from their true loves, and then, under the threat of being thrown into convents, had been forced into unholy marriages' (pp. 415–16). As it is, Rosier is absolutely correct. Because the much-desired union with Warburton has fallen through and because the passionate Rosier still poses a threat to his control over his daughter, Osmond decides to send Pansy to the convent, where, he tells Isabel, '"there is to be nothing ascetic; just to be a certain little sense of sequestration"' (pp. 577–8). Sometimes Osmond's restrained threats are even more disagreeable than his calls for horsewhipping; 'a certain little sense of sequestration' is like 'a mild branding' or 'a brief period on the rack'.

As an American, Osmond is one of those people the psychohistorians warn against: the miserable, kingless republican whose self-rule is quickly exhausted and who must therefore extend his lust for control to the lives of others. This is the same Osmond who says he envies no man save such autocrats as the Czar and the Pope. He is a man of his century, to be sure, but he does not wish to annex Mexico or the Philippines. He wants instead to invade and dominate the women around him: Isabel, Pansy, the masochistic Merle. The one woman Osmond cannot exert his mastery over is the Countess Gemini, whose frivolity is a potent charm against Osmond's humourlessness. Throughout the novel, two sets of words and images are associated with Osmond, the language of imprisonment and that of curatorship. The first suggests the depth of his wickedness; the second keeps the first in check with its banality and thus prevents the melodrama from becoming too overt. (The second language also describes Osmond's everyday reality – he is, after all, an art collector.) What the two languages have in common is that sense of sequestration, of removing something vital from the world to let it gather dust in a cabinet or cell.

As might be expected, the language of imprisonment is central to the meditation in Chapter 42 during which Isabel realizes the enormity of her fate. Indeed, the image of the prison with its clanging doors is made doubly severe because here the prison is underground and thus linked with the premature burial James associated with convent life: Isabel finds 'the infinite vista of a multiplied life to be a dark, narrow alley with a dead wall at the end', an alley leading 'downward and earthward, into realms of restriction and depression where the sound of other lives, easier and freer, was heard as from above, and where it served to deepen the feeling of failure'. Her life in the first year of their marriage seemed bright and airy, but 'then the shadows had begun to gather; it was as if Osmond deliberately, almost malignantly, had put the lights out one by one' (p. 474). This latter image takes on special significance if one is aware of its opposite in the Preface to *The Awkward Age* (1899), where James describes the novelist's benign task as walking around a central subject and turning on a series of lights, 'one by one', until illumination and perfect clarity are achieved.

But Osmond the jailer wants blindness and ignorance for his prisoner; his is 'the house of darkness, the house of dumbness, the house of suffocation', thinks Isabel (p. 478). Everywhere he is associated with the extinction of light. Osmond himself tells Goodwood that he and Isabel are '"as united, you know, as the candlestick and the snuffers"'

(p. 552). When not practising his powers of extinction on Isabel's spirit, he practises them on Pansy's; when Isabel goes to take her leave of Pansy at the convent before returning to England, she thinks that 'she disliked the place, which affronted and almost frightened her; not for the world would she have spent a night there. It produced to-day more than before the impression of a well-appointed prison; for it was not possible to pretend Pansy was free to leave it'. Isabel has been thinking about Madame Merle lately and trying to divine her role in Osmond's life, and when she encounters her nemesis at the convent, she sees her in terms of a striking Gothic image: 'The effect was strange, for Madame Merle was already so present to her vision that her appearance in the flesh was like suddenly, and rather awfully, seeing a painted picture move' (pp. 595–6).

When Isabel visits the dying Ralph, the equivocal nature of her freedom, treated dramatically and imagistically for so many chapters, is once more discussed explicitly. Ralph realizes that, in his own words, he has 'ruined' Isabel; he tells her, ' "You wanted to look at life for yourself – but you were not allowed; you were punished for your wish. You were ground in the very mill of the conventional" ' (pp. 621–2). As before, she gives evidence of what Daniel Schneider (above) calls her 'divided self' and longs for passivity and stasis rather than adventure: 'She envied Ralph his dying, for if one were thinking of rest that was the most perfect of all'. Echoing the Keats who was half in love with easeful death in 'Ode to a Nightingale', she thinks to herself that 'to cease utterly, to give it all up and not know anything more – this idea was as sweet as the vision of a cool bath in a marble tank, in a darkened chamber, in a hot land' (p. 607). In contrast with what Osmond has in mind for her, Isabel's images of self-sequestration – her locking herself in 'the office' of the Albany home, her wanting to be encased in brown holland, and now this one – suggest that retreat is a necessary and even a good idea, but only if one imposes it on oneself.

This idea is strengthened immeasurably in the decisive final confrontation between Isabel and Caspar Goodwood. A careful consideration of that scene will shed new light both on the novel's puzzling end and also the end of melodrama, its search for and ultimate belief in the values it is nonetheless unable to articulate. When he surprises her sitting alone, he is described in language oddly similar to that used to characterize Osmond: 'She had time only to rise when, with a motion that looked like violence, but felt like – she knew not what, he grasped her by the wrist and made her sink again into the seat. She closed her eyes; he had not hurt her; it was only a touch, which she had obeyed. But there was something in his face that she wished not to see. . . . She had a new sensation; he had never produced it before; it was a feeling of danger. . . . The twilight seemed to darken around them' (pp. 631–2). It is easy to say, as some critics have, that Isabel resists Goodwood because she is sexually frigid; certainly there is much in 'his hard manhood' to displease her. But the description of the kiss he forces on her supplies the language to describe exactly what it is that makes her want to escape his embrace. 'His kiss was like white lightning, a flash that spread, and spread again, and stayed. . . . But when darkness returned she was free' (pp. 635–6).

If Osmond wants to practise black magic on Isabel, Goodwood wants to practise white magic. But the point is that Isabel does not want to be entranced by anyone. Given her recent, miserable, still-unresolved enslavement to Osmond, how could any but the most insensitive reader expect her to capitulate thoughtlessly to a new master? Goodwood has the power to possess Isabel, and that power is, if less sinister than the cold tyranny of Osmond, just as insidious for someone who still does not know what freedom is. Isabel breaks the spell of the black magician when she goes to London in defiance of his wishes, and she breaks the spell of the white magician when she proves able to withstand the spell he tries to cast with his kiss.

Moreover, the encounter with Goodwood has caused her to think. Disappointed in the world, Isabel slips into the passive state to which she is so strongly attracted; the narrator tells us that, just before her encounter with Goodwood, 'she lived from day to day, postponing, closing her eyes, trying not to think' (p. 626). Before he kisses her, 'she had not known where to turn', but after, 'she knew now. There was a very straight path' (p. 636). Isabel's decisiveness suggests that, having thought, she has realized that the choice is not between Good-wood and Osmond but between action and inaction. The reader is not told that she is going back to save Pansy, although that is a reasonable assumption; nor is the reader told that she is going back to the protective sequestration of Osmond's house, although one may make a case for that as well. But what the reader sees quite clearly is that she is determined to do *something*. It would not be within the scope of melodramas to say what that something is, but Peter Brooks reminds us that melodrama is fundamentally optimistic, that it does believe that answers are to be found and values affirmed.

The most important characteristic of melodrama is its expressionism, its garrulous belief in words rather than ideas. Perhaps the final word should come from the character in the novel who is, in many ways, the saddest yet the wisest, Madame Merle. Early on she tells Isabel that ' "when you've lived as long as I you'll see that every human being has his shell and that you must take the shell into account. By the shell I mean the whole envelope of circumstances. There's no such thing as an isolated man or woman; we're each of us made up of some cluster of appurtenances" '. This preliminary statement leads to a string of rhetorical questions: ' "what shall we call our 'self'? Where does it begin? where does it end? It overflows into everything that belongs to us – and then it flows back again" '. If this sort of statement seems uncharacteristic for James, it is because his world is largely one of sensibilities; that is to say, it is a material world, not a philosophical one. Yet Merle is proposing a material philosophy: ' "I've a great respect for *things*! One's self – for other people – is one's expression of one's self; and one's house, one's furniture, one's garments, the books one reads, the company one keeps – these things are all expressive" ' (p. 253). The voice is Merle's but it could be that of James the teacher, the writer unaddicted to ideas yet thoroughly committed to the expressive. It takes an older woman to know the nature of the world; after all, Isabel's greatest fault is that, for all that has happened to her, she is still young. And though she tells the dying Ralph Touchett that she feels very old, he tells her, ' "you'll grow young again" ' (p. 623).

The Turn of the Screw

Part One:
Survey

12 Source criticism

Fascinating source studies for *The Turn of the Screw* abound, most of which deal with James's adherence to or departure from Gothic and melodramatic conventions. The specific genesis of the tale, as recounted by James in his Preface to the volume of the New York Edition containing it, is well-known: in January 1895, James heard a story of small children menaced by the spirits of wicked servants on a remote estate; somewhat paradoxically, this account of hellish visitation was related by Edward White Benson, Archbishop of Canterbury. Like the 'germs' or *données* of so many of James's fictions, this one consisted of the merest description of a potentially melodramatic situation and almost no details at all. Indeed, James had something of a reputation among those who knew his work habits for resisting the full account of a story that struck him as having fictional potential and allowing nothing to interfere with his *sui generis* elaboration of it.

One group of source studies deals with the possible impact on James's imagination of the typically lurid magazine illustrations of the day. Robert Lee Wolff suggests that the Archbishop's story may have merged with James's memory of a picture he had surely seen in an 1891 issue of an illustrated London weekly review called *Black and White*. The picture, 'The Haunted House' by one T. Griffiths, continues many of the key elements of the original story; in it, a terrified boy and girl look across a lake at a house with a tower. It is impossible to imagine that James didn't see the picture, since his story 'Sir Edmund Orme' appears in the same issue of *Black and White*. Jean Frantz Blackall posits an even more elaborate connection between James's fiction and magazine art, beginning with James's autobiographical recollection (in *A Small Boy and Others*) of his highly-charged reaction to George Cruikshank's sinister, lurid illustrations of Dickens's *Oliver Twist* (1837–8) and juxtaposing scenes from *The Turn of the Screw* with the appropriate pictures to show how James used Cruikshank's visions of Dickens's world to tap primitive fears of his own.

Leon Edel and Adeline R. Tintner point out that James probably read a tale called *Temptation* that was serialized in *Frank Leslie's New York Journal* in 1855, a story with numerous and striking parallels to *The Turn of the Screw*. Each refers to a fine house in Harley Street; each features significant scenes in courtyards; there are valets, house-keepers, governesses and children aplenty in each; there are similarities in dialogue and phrasing. Most important, the chief villain of *Temptation* is named Peter Quint. This, then, is the use that literary genius makes of popular literature, and to read *Temptation* after having read James's improvement on it, say Edel and Tintner, 'is to hear backward echoes and receive a kind of double-vision of James's imagination in action' (p. 3).

A host of similar studies attempt to position *The Turn of the Screw* in relation solely to the literary tradition. Hans-Joachim Lang observes that while the tale is an unusual one with the Jamesian canon, it is nonetheless technically similar to other examples of Gothicism. *The Turn of the Screw* can be read two ways, one general and allegorical and the other specific and dramatic, as can many tales by Hawthorne. For example, 'The Birthmark' (1846) deals with an alchemist who suspects his wife's birthmark is morally bad for her, but his removal of it proves to be fatal to her. So, too, in James's story: the governess's ethical desire to save the children is commendable yet possibly baseless, whereas her own impact on the children's lives is wrenching and, in Miles's case, fatal. Because James invokes the Gothic tradition by having the governess refer to Ann Radcliffe's *The Mysteries of Udolpho* and Charlotte Brontë's *Jane Eyre*, it isn't a question of whether the ghosts are real or not, says Lang, but whether they belong to the haunted house or to the haunted governess who brings them with her. And either way, the governess is at fault: like Hawthorne's alchemist, she gives hideous reality to what is merely symbolic.

As the source studies for *The Portrait of a Lady* show, James was nothing if not eclectic in his combining of elements both from the popular arts and serious fiction. Regarding *The Turn of the Screw*, many studies demonstrate how James borrowed a single yet telling element from some novel he was familiar with. For example, May L. Ryburn notes that the governess has been reading Fielding's *Amelia*

(1752), which is just the sort of novel that was prohibited in her childhood home, and that there is a connection between her guilty reading and the appearance of the sexually-threatening Quint, who resembles the unsavoury Mr Robinson of *Amelia* so much as to suggest that the ghosts exist only in the governess's mind. Whereas Isabel Archer was an original creation, however, the governess is a socioeconomic type, and invariably the studies of serious fictional sources bring in not only the literary backdrop but also the historical one as well.

Alice Hall Petry considers *The Turn of the Screw* a parody of *Jane Eyre*, noting the numerous similarities (a young woman goes to a remote estate to care for one or more parentless children and there meets a widowed housekeeper who knows of a dark secret, and so on) yet concluding that the traits shared by Jane Eyre and the governess are so exaggerated in the latter that James must have been consciously parodying the Brontë novel and the larger stereotype of the plucky albeit hysterical English governess.

Jane Nardin takes this argument one step farther, stating that '*The Turn of the Screw* can be read as a tale which exposes the cruel and destructive pressures of Victorian society, with its restrictive code of sexual morality and its strong sense of class consciousness, upon a group of basically sane and decent individuals' (pp. 151–2). Even though *The Turn of the Screw* is touted as a ghost story, it has not one or two but three potential love affairs thwarted by class distinctions, affairs involving the love of the narrator Douglas for the governess, the governess for the master, and Quint for Jessel. The attendant frustrations warp the lives of everyone in the story. For example, because Quint and Jessel cannot marry, Miles and Flora become the children they cannot have legitimately, just as the servants become the parents of the orphaned children. Nardin locates the crux of the satori in Miles's expulsion from school: if Miles has been speaking approvingly of relations between different classes, he is striking at his school's *raison d'être*, which is to prepare status-conscious gentlemen to take their places in a hierarchical society. The youthful governess, who was probably raised in the fundamentalist Evangelical wing of the Church of England, can only see the issue in terms of good and evil, and therefore she invents the ghost, making *The Turn of the Screw* not a story of madness, however, but of a rigid social milieu and its distorting effects on the people who live in it.

As opposed to Petry and Nardin, Elliot M. Scherero also puts the governess within a Victorian frame of reference yet views her approvingly as a result. *The Turn of the Screw* acquires most of its ambiguity after the First World War thanks to critics influenced by the growth of psychoanalysis and, after the Second by 'a general preoccupation with interpretation' (p. 261). Victorians, however, would have been influenced by their own reading to see the story more clearly. They would have seen in it one more tale of the corruption of children by the lower classes, as spelled out in the writings of Maria Edgeworth, William Godwin, Mrs Henry Sherwood, Anne Brontë, Lady Violet Greville, and James Mark Baldwin. They would have seen also that the governess had arrived to save the children. So while 'to some twentieth-century critics she is a monster of suspicion who leaves Miles and Flora no peace ... [to] most Victorians, however, she will have demonstrated a proper concern for the moral welfare of her pupils' (p. 269). Quint and Jessel are 'nightmare parodies' of good servants who try to 'undo the training required for membership in the higher classes' (p. 273). If the governess is ineffectual against them, then the story is a frightening one indeed – she represents civilization arrayed against the forces of evil, yet she cannot win.

A final group of source studies focuses on James's familiarity with contemporary 'scientific' literature on ghostly apparitions. A pioneer in this field is Francis X. Roellinger, Jr., who points out that James's discussion of ghostly sightings in the Preface to *The Turn of the Screw* suggests that he was familiar with the reports of the Society for Psychical Research, and that the ghosts in the tale 'are conceived to a surprising extent in terms of the cases reported to the Society' (p. 405). Thus, whereas the ghost of the Gothic tradition is fearsome, shroud-draped, burdened by chains, and punctual (it always appears at midnight), the 'new' ghost looks as it did when alive, wears the same clothes, is silent, and may show up any time in any place. A full-length study by Peter Beidler argues exhaustively that 'Henry James knew the people who were at the very center of certain controversies about ghosts and demons, that he had read widely in the published books and articles about such subjects, and that he was careful to write *The Turn of the Screw* in such a way that it would have sounded realistic to those at least generally familiar with spiritualism and psychical research' (p. 16). Before the reader descends into the seemingly ceaseless maelstrom of critical opinion regarding the ghosts' reality and the governess's sanity, it is good to recognize that James was writing for a highly-informed and well-read audience for whom such questions were far from settled. Engaging complex epistemological and moral issues in all their ambiguity, *The Turn of the Screw* is an ideal vehicle for the workings of the melodramatic mind.

13 New criticism (apparitionist)

To date, almost every interpretation of *The Turn of the Screw* takes either the apparitionist stance (the ghosts are real, the governess sane) or the non-apparitionist (the ghosts are unreal, figments of the governess's diseased imagination). Many source studies (above) argue for an apparitionist reading, and while it is an oversimplification to say that all interpretative studies which argue for the ghosts' reality are New Critical in nature, it is a fact that most of them are, either entirely or in part. Non-apparitionist readers often tend to be psychological critics; if the governess can be proved insane, one need not argue the reality of the ghosts. Conversely, if the ghosts *are* real, the best way to prove it is through the New Critical technique of linking myriad bits of evidence to reveal a central and incontrovertible truth that has nothing to do with any individual's perception.

Since the New Criticism is associated most frequently with the close reading of poetry, it is fitting that Robert Heilman treat *The Turn of the Screw* as a well-made poem, a text in which the author grafts 'a tantalizing body of suggestion' onto 'the every-day [sic] commonplaces of fictional method' (p. 187). At the beginning, numerous analogies are drawn between Bly and Eden; when Quint first appears, the estate is 'stricken with death'; the seasons change, the foliage withers, and a time of darkness and storms descends. And if Bly is Eden, Miles and Flora are portrayed as 'the childhood of the race. They are symbolic children as the ghosts are symbolic ghosts' (p. 178). 'James has an almost religious sense of the duality of man, and ... he makes that sense explicit in terms broadly religious and even Christian' (p. 181). Thus *The Turn of the Screw* is 'a morality play, but in a complicated, enriched, and intensified version' (p. 184). And therefore the governess is a priest, the pastor of a flock, as she makes clear when she tells Miles she wants him to help her to save him. In effect, hers is a 'lay mind with a religious sense' that is grappling with 'the doctrine of original sin ... but without precise theological tools' (p. 185). She fails, of course, and we are left with 'a modern late-fall defeat patterned on the ancient springtide victory – a 'Black Easter', as it were (p. 187). For the moral stakes to be so high and the literary complications to be worthwhile, clearly the ghosts must be real.

Alexander E. Jones's study of the evidence for the ghosts' existence is a classic New Critical close reading of the text in which he focuses on three incidents: (1) Mrs Grose's identification of Quint from the governess's detailed description of his appearance; (2) Mrs Grose's confirmation of Flora's shocking utterance and thus the ghosts' corrupting effect on the children; and (3) Miles's naming Peter Quint at the last even though the governess has never mentioned him to the children. These points have been raised by other critics, but the virtue of Jones's arguments is that, in every case, he presents the non-appari-tionists' counterarguments and then disproves them; the result is an engaging conversation between critical schools rather than a series of mere assertions. As for those who say that nothing in the story can be accepted as true since it all comes from the governess, Jones observes that no narrator can deceive the reader permanently. If that were the case, all great literature may be dismissed out of hand – Huckleberry Finn never drifted down the Mississippi, and *Moby-Dick* is just a hoax perpetrated by Ishmael on a bunch of gullible landlubbers.

Like Jones, Oliver Evans argues with the non-apparitionists, taking them on point by point. For example, where the psychological critics argue that the governess must be mad because she alone sees the ghosts, Evans points out that this is not only traditional but also represents a definite victory for the ghosts, who want to defeat the governess, after all, and not simply run wild on the estate. As for the heroine's reliability, 'one could not . . . wish for stronger evidence of the stability of the governess's personality than the fact that, although her housekeeper herself has seen nothing, she does not doubt that her friend has – a point which James, who certainly sees the necessity for it, drives home again and again' (p. 206).

In his consideration of *The Turn of the Screw*, Charles G. Hoffman glances briefly at other James novels before getting into the text proper. He notes that to James evil is usually an aspect of social conduct and can appear as infidelity (*The Portrait of a Lady*, *The Golden Bowl*), betrayal (*The Wings of the Dove*), and even lack of taste (*The Spoils of Poynton*). *The Turn of the Screw*, on the other hand, is the only James fiction in which innocence versus evil is the central conflict; James takes pains to write his story on those terms, which is why it is crucial that innocence and evil are real, i.e., that the governess is not

insane. The frame story helps in this respect: the solid and stable
Douglas establishes the governess as 'a Jane Austen character of
romantic sensibility' rather than 'a Freudian personality of repressed sexuality' (p. 215). In the first two chapters, the governess's
normalcy is established (were she a traditional hysteric, she would
have been one from the beginning). And like Douglas, the sensible
Grose functions as a corroborator by believing in the ghost as much as
the governess does, at least until the lakeside scene in Chapters 19
and 20; however, it is well-established in ghostly lore that ghosts
appear to some viewers but not others. As with other James novels of
the period, innocence is presented as a lack of the knowledge of evil.
'One of the basic ironies of the novel', writes Hoffman, 'is that the
governess, in the role of protectress, causes evil to come out in the
open; it is to her that the ghosts first appear, and it is her over-
developed sense of duty that is the very means by which the children's
corruption is revealed'. Thus 'her high sense of duty leads her, like
Oedipus, to seek the truth, a course that can only lead to her destruc-
tion' (p. 221). What virtually all the apparitionist critics object to
most in the neurotic case-study approach is its reductionist nature,
which is why the emphasis in these largely New Critical essays tends
to be on theme, either the philosophical one of appearance versus
reality or the ethical one of good versus evil or both.

14 Psychological criticism (non-apparitionist)

Edna Kenton is widely credited with being the first to go on record
saying that the ghosts 'are only exquisite dramatizations of [the
governess's] little personal mystery, figures for the ebb and flow of
troubled thought within her mind, acting out her story' (pp. 113–14).
Her essay is dated in its critical method, since it merely asserts that
the governess is mad without arguing the point evidentially, as a New
Critical study would. On the other hand, Kenton is surprisingly
contemporary in her insistence that the reader must complete the
picture that James has outlined.
    Edmund Wilson begins his essay by acknowledging Kenton's, and
his name is often linked with hers whenever pioneering non-apparitionist work is mentioned. He soon goes considerably beyond his
predecessor, however, in finding *The Turn of the Screw* to be 'a neurotic
case of sex repression' similar to ones detailed in *The Bostonians*

(1886), *The Sacred Fount* (1901), *The Tragic Muse* (1890), and other works. This essay proceeds along classic Freudian lines, and to Wilson goes the distinction of noting that Quint appears on a phallic tower and Jessel by a yonic lake and that at one point Flora is seen tightening one piece of wood into another in a simulation of sexual intercourse. His overall argument is that the fiction of James's early career is sexless; then, after the theatrical débâcle culminating in *Guy Domville* (1895), sex appears, but as an irregular, illicit, even obsessive force; and it is only with *The Awkward Age* that moral values begin to reassert themselves as James establishes himself once again as a writer of the first rank.

Revising this essay for book publication in 1948, though, Wilson felt compelled to note that not only is the governess self-deceived but so is her creator, who wants to protect his heroine despite her obvious guilt. Astonishing as it may seem, Wilson changed his mind yet again, adding a note in 1959 arguing that James knew precisely what he was doing and intended to show that the governess was delusional, as indicated by his including *The Turn of the Screw* in the same volume of the 1907 New York Edition that held 'The Aspern Papers' and 'The Liar', both of which feature narrators who falsify reports of their own actions.

The beauty of literary criticism lies in the different, even opposing meanings that can be derived from a given aspect of a story, and if numerous New Critics see the governess's calm logic as a sign of her rationality, as many psychological critics see this same quality as a mask of restraint forced upon a volatile nature. For example, Muriel West notes that the 'serene, dignified dialogue' of the governess cannot completely obscure her 'nervous excitement and rash physical activity' (p. 341). Though her talk is calm, she describes herself as springing up, moving blindly, falling against furniture, trembling, seizing Flora so forcefully that the child cries out in pain and fright, and holding Miles's feverish, sweaty body so tightly that she can feel his heart beat. So one may say that the governess 'indulges in an exuberant debauch of violence' or at least dreams she does. Her actions recall Spencer Brydon's wild desire to clutch something when he encounters the ghost in 'The Jolly Corner' (1908) as well as James's description in *A Small Boy and Others* of the childhood dream in which he routs a vague yet formidable foe, using 'the words *act, rush, bound, inspired, triumph, visitant*, much as the governess does' and revealing 'a delight, an elation, a joy in the adventure almost identical with hers' (p. 348). *The demonic ghosts are a threat to a. as well as children*

If the New Critics are able to take the high philosophical and moral ground in their lofty assessments of themes, psychological critics have the advantage of greater lateral movement among the myriad personality quirks of the main character and others, as the following three essays demonstrate. Harold C. Goddard is unique in considering the world of *The Turn of the Screw* from the viewpoint of the two children, beginning with his own experience. As a boy, Goddard and his sister were cared for by an insane servant who, though good-natured and affectionate, used to tell stories of dead people who visited her during the night. 'This woman did not long remain a servant in our family', writes Goddard. 'But suppose she had! Suppose our parents had died, or, for some other reason, we had been placed exclusively in her care. . . . What might have happened to us? What might not!' (p. 257). From his own feelings, Goddard is able to extrapolate explanations for the seemingly bizarre but ultimately quite natural behaviour of the children, for example, the shriek that Miles emits when the governess falls on her knees and begs him to let her save him, a natural response on his part but one she attributes to the only cause she can conceive of, ghostly possession. (In a prefatory note to this essay, Leon Edel speculates that it was written around 1920, or before Edna Kenton's study, though it was not published for nearly forty years, and then posthumously; thus Goddard appears to be the first to expound, if not publish, a non-apparitionist reading.)

Walter Stepp's imaginative reading of *The Turn of the Screw* begins by linking Miles and Douglas (each had a younger sister as well as a governess ten years older than himself, a duplication that could have hardly slipped by the Henry James who was almost boastful in his pride of craft) and then proceeds to an analysis of the frame rather than the story proper. Specifically, Stepp isolates the image one of the house guests offers of a ghost story he has heard of a frightened boy who wakes his mother so she can see the apparition that has come to terrify him. The mention of this incident is what prompts Douglas – or Miles Douglas, as Stepp calls him – to tell his own. Why? Because his too is the story of an extraordinary love, that of a boy for a kind, unhappy, deluded woman he loved as a son would love a mother.

Finally, an essay by C. Knight Aldrich rivals *The Turn of the Screw* itself for imaginative achievement and is so deliciously revealing of the possibilities of interpretation that one stands in awe of even its most farfetched implications. Aldrich speculates that, because the governess not only assumes the authority of (as well as authority over) Mrs Grose as well as her place in the children's hearts, the reader may assume that Mrs Grose 'not only hates the governess but, in an effort to destroy her, supports and encourages her belief in the existence of a sinister component in what was really no more than a casual relationship between the children and two employees' (p. 368). Further, the presumed death of the children's parents seems handled almost negligently and may suggest a cover-up of the children's illegitimacy; the uncle's generous support of Miles and Flora yet abhorrence of contact with them suggests an understandable combination of obligation and guilt. And if the uncle is the father, the mother is none other than Mrs Grose, who agrees with the governess that the master of Bly likes young and pretty women but not those who have lost their youth and beauty. Aldrich says that James did not make this clear either because he overestimated his readers or because 'Mrs. Grose may have represented his mother, in reality a destructive woman, but a woman of whom James was so afraid that he had to repress his perception of her evil characteristics and consciously could only see her as good' (p. 373). Psychology becomes tragedy in Aldrich's hands; his account of *The Turn of the Screw* has an evil older woman driving an unstable younger woman completely out of her mind yet causing the inadvertent death of her own son.

15 Post-new criticism

Structuralism, an analytical method introduced to anthropology by Claude Lévi-Strauss but used in literary criticism as well, assumes repetitive phenomena reveal unconscious but consistent laws in everything from the lives of primitive peoples to the works of novelists and poets. Tobin Siebers's structuralist study of *The Turn of the Screw* begins with Tzvetan Todorov's assertion that narratives dealing with the supernatural should be read in terms of their use of the concept of hesitation. James's tale is filled with hesitations and then headlong plunges on the part of the governess, actions paralleled by the reader who judges the governess sane and the ghosts real (or vice versa) by 'excluding chaotic elements', which is what tribal societies do when they make myths (p. 568).

But on a more sophisticated level, says Siebers, this primitive 'logic of exclusion' must be denied and the story allowed to thrive as pure text. 'More than a simple game, *The Turn of the Screw* dares the reader to examine the logic of exclusion and hesitation.... The reader may choose to hesitate once more over the [ghosts], governess, or children; or he may choose to hesitate over hesitation.... If he chooses to hesitate over either the governess or the children, he affirms the founding opposition of the story's underlying mythology and falls into James's well-laid trap. If he chooses to hesitate over hesitation and to recognize the occurrence of a radical discontinuity, he allows literature to teach him what literature is' (pp. 571–2).

In his deconstructive reading of the tale, Kevin Murphy, like Siebers, faults the reader who simply picks one of the two interpretative possibilities and then refuses to consider any evidence to the contrary; though his critical method differs, Murphy too argues for the ultimate opacity of the narrative and he examines the strategies that James uses to make a single consistent reading impossible. Murphy turns the text against itself in the classic deconstructive way, emphasizing the collaboration between speaker and listener (Douglas and narrator, governess and Mrs Grose, author and reader) in which one is prodded and encouraged to agree with and elaborate upon suggestions made by another. In this way, the narrative grows simultaneously richer and less real, until it offers no more assurance than the images in an Impressionist painting which exist only in the eye of the beholder.

The term 'post-structural criticism' is sometimes used as a synonym for deconstruction, but whereas the latter is usually characterized by an almost formulaic display of opposites within a text that prevents the emergence of meaning, post-structuralism generally takes a broader, more eclectic approach that includes deconstructive principles but can use concepts from psychoanalysis and elsewhere. Darrel Mansell proposes three chronological stages of *The Turn of the Screw* criticism: one that believed there were ghosts at Bly, a second asserting that the ghosts were in the mind of the governess, and the present one which finds the ghosts in the language of the text itself. In her use of such painterly terms as 'stroke by stroke', 'a touch of picture', 'picture in a frame', and 'portrait', the governess seems 'to be writing not *about* her subject but to be writing the subject itself', as evidenced by her saying that, at Quint's first appearance, 'I saw him as I see the letters I form on this page' (pp. 56–8). Many of the ghosts in the text are pronouns with mistaken referents or none at all; at times the characters are unsure whether 'he' refers to Miles or Quint and 'she' to Miss Jessel or the governess. The most important of these vague pronouns, of course, is the 'you' in Miles's outburst 'Peter Quint – you devil!' Because the reader will never know whether Miles is referring to Quint or the governess, says Mansell, 'the "you" scared up into life inhabits not Bly but the *text* – a ghost in the text' (p. 60). So the text spirals inward, leaving behind the great world (Douglas's estate, Harley Street, Bly) and even the governess's own mind and ends up describing itself; if it is a picture, it is one in which its inhabitants are trapped, unable to describe whatever reality they inhabit.

Post-New Critical psychoanalytical criticism differs so much from the earlier variety that it is almost as though there were two Freuds: an earlier, positivistic scientist who found a one-to-one correlation between dream images and neurotic tendencies and a later, tentative philosopher who realized that the delicate relation between analyst and analysand was governed as much by his own perceptions as by anything the patient said. Thus a latter-day Freudian like Shoshana Felman regards Edmund Wilson's early effort (above) as an oversimplified search for a single interpretation of *The Turn of the Screw*. Felman considers the story's text equivalent to a patient's unconscious mind: it is locked away and must be sent for, and when it arrives, the text turns out to be a story of letters that the reader can never read – the one from Miles's school announcing his dismissal, the children's letters to their uncle that the governess intercepts, her own letter to him which is intercepted by Miles. Having been sent for, this story about reading the unreadable arrives as an unreadable letter itself and thus ends up as a trap for the reader. The law of *The Turn of the Screw* is flight and escape, and everyone in charge manages to get away: the master of Bly escapes and becomes a kind of ghost hovering in the margins, and so does an equivocal Henry James who refuses to tell us what to believe. At the end, no one is left except the reader, sitting in a circle around the fire of the frame story and trying to read the letter-manuscript. 'As the fire within the letter is reflected on our faces', says Felman, 'we see the very madness of our own art staring back at us. In thus mystifying us so as to demystify our errors and our madness, it is we ourselves that James makes laugh – and bleed. The joke is indeed on us; the worry, ours' (p. 207).

Marxist critics often have little sympathy with deconstructionists, post-structuralists, psychoanalytic critics, and other 'ironic' readers whose commentaries seem to encourage fatalism and passivity. To Bruce Robbins, *The Turn of the Screw* is not about inescapable linguistic traps at all but about the very real problem of sex between the classes, specifically, between the children and the ghosts and between the governess and the master. The problem is never solved because the governess, who desires the master, can never bring herself to admit that the ghosts, who have similar desires toward the children, are mirror images of herself. The story builds toward a happy ending that never arrives, one in which class distinctions are removed and Bly becomes the Eden that it seemed to be when the governess first saw it.

Part Two:
Appraisal

16 A mid-life crisis

With 'Daisy Miller', *Roderick Hudson*, *The American*, and *The Portrait of a Lady*, not to mention a handful of additional volumes, including short fiction, travel essays and criticism, James completed what might have been an entire career for a lesser artist. Had he stopped with *The Portrait of a Lady*, Henry James would still be thought of as a novelist of the first rank; certainly that novel alone would have guaranteed him a rank in the canon higher than that of, say, Howells or Trollope.

But James was destined by his art for something greater. The problem was that he was not ready for further greatness, not yet. First, something had to happen, even if he had to make it happen himself. What James did was to devote precious years of his life to the writing of plays that somehow managed to be stiff and maudlin at the same time; worse, he wrote them for the venerable London stage, the stage of Shakespeare and (even more worrisome) Oscar Wilde. Playwriting represented to James something comparable to what the writing of screenplays means to serious novelists of the present day: a chance to make much more money than one might by writing for a reading élite and to get much more name recognition. In the 1880s, James felt neglected and underrated by his reading public, such as it was, so he took up the false pen of the playwright and betrayed the art he had spent so much time perfecting.

James's career in the theatre came to smash on the evening of 5 January 1895, the day of the opening of *Guy Domville*. Too nervous to see his own play and perhaps prescient of its failure, the novelist went to the nearby Haymarket Theatre to see Oscar Wilde's new play, *An Ideal Husband*, before walking over to the St James's Theatre, where *Guy Domville* was just ending calamitously. In contrast to the sparkling epigrams of Wilde's play, James's told the lugubrious story of a young man torn between continuing his family line and taking holy orders. The impatient audience found amusement in, among other things, the over-elaborate costume of the actress playing the dowager Mrs Domville; their tittering unnerved the actors, and the deteriorating production encouraged the audience to even greater displays of dissatisfaction. When the actor playing Guy Domville said 'I'm the *last*, my lord, of the Domvilles', a voice from the gallery replied, 'It's a bloody good thing you are'. In what may have been a state of simple distraction or an actual fit of pique, George Alexander, the actor-manager who played the lead role, led James onstage, where, as he later reported to his brother William, the audience roared at him like beasts in a zoo.

According to Brooks, it was a simple matter of writing for the wrong stage: James was immersed in and deeply admiring of the French melodramatic tradition, and if *Guy Domville* had appeared in Paris rather than London, no doubt it would have fared better. Regardless, James's theatrical years were a period of self-betrayal, redeemed partly by his use of dramatic techniques in the novels he wrote in the late 1890s and thereafter.

But the theatrical experiment may have served another, greater purpose. It may have caused James to halt one line of development so that he could begin another with greater potential. Critics are fond of pointing out how anomalous *The Turn of the Screw* is, how dissimilar it is to anything else he wrote. However, what if *The Turn of the Screw* were not a mid-career quirk but the first fiction of a wholly new career, yet one largely parallel to the career he had already completed? Some minor work aside, the first career begins with *The American*, an overt melodrama, and ends with *The Portrait of a Lady*, a covert one; the second begins with the overtly melodramatic *The Turn of the Screw* and concludes with the covert melodrama of *The Wings of the Dove*. Even plot and thematic elements are similar: both *The American* and *The Turn of the Screw* treat innocent characters who discover too late that good intentions are not enough. And *The Portrait of a Lady* and *The Wings of the Dove* are even more alike: in each, an adorable, fabulously wealthy American girl goes to Italy (after having turned down a marriage proposal from an English lord), where she is victimized by a man and a woman who have schemed against her.

One thing that is common to all of James's writing is his consistent use of the materials of melodrama. Even a passing acquaintance with

The Portrait of a Lady is enough for one to see there a basic melodramatic situation: a beautiful and worthy female 'prisoner' deceived and held captive by an unscrupulous male 'jailer' who even lives in more than one jail-like house. In *The Turn of the Screw*, Bly is as Gothic as any of Gilbert Osmond's residences, but it is harder to say who is good and who is not. Even at her most menaced, the governess is clearly the jailer – it is her desire to be in charge, and she takes great pride in doing so. But whereas it was clear in *The Portrait of a Lady* that Osmond was a sort of black magician and Caspar Goodwood a white, it is impossible to say whether the governess is on the side of the devils or the angels. But then melodrama need not articulate values, only search for them.

17   The jailer

As Douglas points out in the frame story, the inexperienced governess, just twenty years old and taking up her first post, goes from having no power to having it absolutely. Nervous, impressionable, she leaves the rigid environment of her poor clergyman-father's home to work for a man who tells her, as Douglas recounts, 'that she should never trouble him – but never, never: neither appeal nor complain nor write about anything; only meet all questions herself, receive all moneys from his solicitor, take the whole thing over and let him alone' (p. 151). The governess the reader meets is both possessing and possessed. Immediately upon meeting Flora, she refers to her as 'my little girl'; a sentence later, she says that 'there had been a moment when I believed I recognised, faint and far, the cry of a child; there had been another when I found myself just consciously starting as at the passage, before my door, of a light footstep' (p. 153). The ghostly apparitions proliferate, of course, but what is less noticeable is the governess's fondness for the possessive pronoun. Again and again she refers to '"my pupils"', '"*my* boy"', and, at the harrowing realization that she has lost the children to the ghosts, '"they're not mine – they're not ours. They're his and they're hers!"' (pp. 176, 177, 207).

Like Isabel Archer and the other divided selves of James's fiction, as Daniel Schneider has called them, the governess wants to dominate and be dominated. Chapter 1 of *The Turn of the Screw* concludes on both notes almost simultaneously, with the governess telling Mrs Grose that she is '"rather easily carried away"', that she was '"carried away in London"' (that is, on meeting the handsome master of Bly), yet on the 'great drifting ship' that is Bly, she finds herself 'strangely at the helm' (pp. 154–6).

A metaphor used consistently throughout that is appropriate to the governess's self-division (as well as reminiscent of James's theatrical débâcle) is that of acting. The actor, after all, is both controlled and controlling: bound by the limits of the play, she nonetheless has the potential – indeed, the professional imperative – to spellbind her audience. As autumn settles on Bly and the ghosts become more menacing, she thinks that 'the place, with its grey sky and withered garlands, its bared spaces and scattered dead leaves, was like a theatre after the performance – all strewn with crumpled playbills', and when she thinks of confronting the children about the existence of the ghosts, she says that 'at odd moments, I shut myself up audibly to rehearse . . . the manner in which I might come to the point' (pp. 211, 213). In fact, versions of this same metaphor appear so frequently in James's fiction as to suggest not only his love of and desire to succeed in the theatre but also the one idea that is perhaps essential to all of his writing: that of the individual struggling to create a persona while simultaneously bound and free.

When the governess is threatened with possession, she threatens to possess: her functional similarity to the ghosts is suggested most strongly in Chapter 4, when Quint peers in through the dining room window to startle her and she routs him by rushing outside and taking his place, startling Mrs Grose in turn when she peers in exactly as Quint did. Like Isabel, the governess is proud. Chapter 6 contains an almost rhapsodic burst of self-congratulation in which she realizes 'the extraordinary flight of heroism', the 'magnificent chance' that will allow her 'to succeed where many another girl might have failed'; later, she acknowledges the erotic stimulus which prompts her to endanger her mission even as she pretends to fulfil it when she refers to 'the fine machinery I had set in motion to attract [the master's] attention to my slighted charms' (pp. 179, 208). The difference between Isabel and the governess is that the former was surrounded by any number of well-meaning confidants whereas the latter has only Mrs Grose, who is hardly prepared to check her reckless disregard of the children. In a portentous moment of self-revelation, the governess says that Mrs Grose 'offered her mind to my disclosures as, had I wished to mix a witch's broth and proposed it with assurance, she would have held out a large clean saucepan' (p. 203). What makes the governess so different from James's other characters is the degree to which she is free to create difficulties for herself and others.

She accedes to her passive side in Chapter 15, when, feeling that she can tolerate the situation no longer, she resolves to free herself of the prison Bly has become. While the others are at church, she returns to the house to pack, but on seeing Miss Jessel there, she realizes that she must stay and save the children. She sets about doing so in the only sensible way possible, which is to write to the master and enlist his aid. But before her letter can be sent, she finds she cannot resist the temptation to wring a confession out of Miles, 'to seize once more the chance of possessing him' (p. 228). Chapter 17 ends with a typically ambiguous moment of possessing/possession: either Miles shrieks because Quint has entered the room in the form of a gust of cold air and an earthquake-like shaking or because he is simply terrified at the governess's controlling mania.

It is at this point in the story that the governess's behaviour becomes most manipulative, lending encouragement to those who believe her to be a demented schemer (although her devotees will insist that she is merely taking extraordinary measures to save the children); in Chapter 18, for example, she tells outright lies to Mrs Grose, saying that Miss Jessel has taken Flora while Quint and Miles are together in the schoolroom. But if the governess is reaching a peak of infernal (or angelic) bravado, so are the other characters. Flora, who is wandering by the lake, 'smiled as if her performance had now become complete', and in fact the crucial scene that follows is played out very much like a theatrical production (p. 236). In a fully-developed play, the players are not only controlled by the text and their own impulses but also by the other actors, and so it is here. The governess finds Flora 'prepared and on her guard'; she refuses to acknowledge the presence of Miss Jessel and instead will 'not even feign to glance in the direction' of the dead rival 'but only, instead of that, turn at *me* an expression of hard still gravity, an expression absolutely new and unprecedented and that appeared to read and accuse and judge me'. The governess loses to Miss Jessel, who has written the scene the way she wants it. ' "Of course I've lost you" ', she says to Flora, ' "I've interfered, and you've seen, under *her* dictation ... the easy and perfect way to meet it" ' (pp. 239, 241).

Defeated in her attempt to possess Flora, to prevent her possession by Miss Jessel, the governess feels her circumstances closing around her: 'it was a tighter place still than I had yet turned round in', she confides at the beginning of Chapter 22. Her only hope now is to possess Miles and, by so doing, vindicate her extraordinary aggression ('for if he *were* innocent what then on earth was I?' [p. 260]). The language of their final confrontation is the typical language of control and possession in James: 'I let him go', 'he was soon at some distance from me', '"*I* have you"', 'I caught him ... I held him' (pp. 260–2). At the last, what she holds is a corpse – 'dispossessed', as she says. But dispossessed of whom? Miles has fled the prison of life, but no one can say who has been his jailer. The story which seems likely to end with a revelation, simply ends.

18   The uses of melodrama

The first use of melodrama, to quote Levy, is that it serves as 'the means by which James infuses his most deeply felt moral concerns with a sense of peril and crisis' (p. 116). Melodrama looks back toward the Gothic tradition with its pure damsels, evil villains and sinister mansions. In melodrama, the suffering is horrible; in *The Portrait of a Lady* and *The Turn of the Screw*, it seems to be endless. Perhaps this is necessary. Perhaps the heroines must suffer so that we may not. Were they to be anything other than sacrificial, the evil they nullify through sacrifice might be vented on such weaker figures as ourselves. When old Daniel Touchett says, '"The ladies can save us"', he may be saying that they can only do so at a tremendous price to themselves. (It goes without saying that James created many long-suffering male characters as well.)

But if melodrama looks back to Gothicism, it looks forward to the thinking of Freud, and not so much the 'new', tentative Freud of post-modern philosophers and critics but the 'old' one who thought he could banish unhappiness through scientific means. In Gothic novels, villains are external; in psychoanalysis, one's own unconscious is often the traitor. 'The talking cure' is more often a rescue, not of the speaker, but of the listener, who can at least say, 'I'll not make *that* mistake!' Douglas seems to be disburdening himself of something terribly weighty as he prepares to read the governess's story, and, in like manner, the reader of Henry James's fiction is cured, at least for the moment, of the disease of ordinary living.

The so-called Master Thinkers of the 1960s, such as Louis Althusser, Jacques Lacan and Michel Foucault (as well as their respective predecessors Marx, Freud and Nietzsche) have in common the argument that humanism is largely dead, that we are controlled by the impersonal structures of class struggle or psychology or language. But as Paul Berman points out, in recent months there has been a critique of the Master Thinkers by the younger French critics (such as Luc Ferry, Alain Renault, Alain Finkielkraut and Pascal Bruckner) who find their ways of viewing culture obscurantist and despotic and who, instead, urge a viewpoint akin to Enlightenment humanism with its belief in mass education, shared values and political progress. A seemingly hoary genre like melodrama may be precisely suited for such an undertaking; perhaps melodrama is the genre of the future as well as the past.

Melodrama cures by its 'urging toward combat in life', as Brooks says; 'it works to steel man for resistance, it keeps him going in the face of threat' (p. 206). Moreover, it does so with the utmost in intellectual courage, for it offers no false promises. Of course James wanted happiness or at least freedom from care. But when he took up his pen, he did so to find his own salvation, not in his creations, but in his creating.

References and Further Reading

Bibliographic information is given on each item mentioned in the surveys of criticism of *The Portrait of a Lady* (Part One) and *The Turn of the Screw* (Part One).

The Portrait of a Lady (Part One)

1 Source criticism

Beauchamp, Andrea Roberts, '"Isabel Archer": A Possible Source for *The Portrait of a Lady*', *American Literature*, 49 (1977), pp. 267–71.

Leavis, F. R., *The Great Tradition* (New York, 1963).

Levine, George, 'Isabel, Gwendolyn, and Dorothea', *ELH*, 30 (1963), pp. 244–57.

Long, Robert Emmet, *The Great Succession: Henry James and the Legacy of Hawthorne* (Pittsburgh, 1979).

Nettels, Elsa, '*The Portrait of a Lady* and the Gothic Romance', *South Atlantic Bulletin*, 39 (1974), pp. 73–82.

Tribble, Joseph L., 'Cherbuliez's *Le Roman d'une Honnête Femme*: Another Source of James's *The Portrait of a Lady*', *American Literature*, 40 (1968), pp. 279–93.

2 Textual criticism

Baym, Nina, 'Revision and Thematic Change in *The Portrait of a Lady*', *Modern Fiction Studies*, 22 (1976), pp. 183–200.

Mazzella, Anthony J., 'James's *The Portrait of a Lady*', *The Explicator*, 30 (1972), item 30.

Mazzella, Anthony J., 'The New Isabel', in *The Portrait of a Lady* (ed.) Robert D. Bamberg (New York, 1975).

3 Technical and structural criticism

Collins, Martha, 'The Narrator, the Satellites, and Isabel Archer: Point of View in *The Portrait of a Lady*', *Studies in the Novel*, 8 (1976), pp. 142–57.
Daiches, David, 'Sensibility and Technique: Preface to a Critique', *Kenyon Review*, 5 (1943), pp. 569–79.
Feidelson, Charles, 'The Moment of *The Portrait of a Lady*', *Ventures*, 8 (1968), pp. 47–55.
Liebman, Sheldon W., 'Point of View in *The Portrait of a Lady*', *English Studies*, 52 (1971), pp. 136–47.
Westervelt, Linda A., ' "The Growing Complexity of Things": Narrative Technique in *The Portrait of a Lady*', *Journal of Narrative Technique*, 13 (1983), pp. 74–85.

4 New criticism (image)

Anderson, Charles R., *Person, Place, and Thing in Henry James* (Durham, 1977).
Frederick, John T., 'Patterns of Imagery in Chapter 42 of Henry James's *The Portrait of a Lady*', *Arizona Quarterly*, 25 (1969), pp. 150–6.
Rodenbeck, John, 'The Bolted Door in James's *Portrait of a Lady*', *Modern Fiction Studies*, 10 (1964–5), pp. 330–40.
Williams, Paul O., 'James's *The Portrait of a Lady*', *The Explicator*, 22 (1964), item 50.
Winner, Viola Hopkins, *Henry James and the Visual Arts* (Charlottesville, 1969).

5 New criticism (character)

Blodgett, Harriet, 'Verbal Clues in *The Portrait of a Lady*: A Note in Defense of Isabel Archer', *Studies in American Fiction*, 7 (1979), pp. 27–36.

Krook, Dorothea, *The Ordeal of Consciousness in Henry James* (Cambridge, 1967).

Liebman, Sheldon W., 'The Light and the Dark: Character Design in the Portrait of a Lady', *Papers in Language and Literature*, 6 (1970), pp. 163–79.

Schneider, Daniel, *The Crystal Cage: Adventures of the Imagination in the Fiction of Henry James* (Lawrence, 1978).

Stallman, Robert W., *The Houses That James Built* (East Lansing, 1961).

Wagenknecht, Edward, *Eve and Henry James* (Norman, 1978).

Weinstein, Philip M., *Henry James and the Requirements of the Imagination* (Cambridge, 1971).

6   New criticism (theme)

Kleinberg, Seymour, 'Ambiguity and Ambivalence: The Psychology of Sexuality in Henry James's *The Portrait of a Lady*', *Markham Review*, 5 (1969), pp. 2–7.

Powers, Lyall H., '*The Portrait of a Lady*: The Eternal Mystery of Things', *Nineteenth-Century Fiction*, 14 (1959), pp. 143–55.

Sicker, Philip, *Love and the Quest for Identity in the Fiction of Henry James* (Princeton, 1980).

7   Post-new criticism

Allen, Elizabeth, '*The Portrait of a Lady*', in *A Woman's Place in the Novels of Henry James* (Macmillan, 1984); reprinted in *Henry James's The Portrait of a Lady* (ed.) Harold Bloom (New York, 1987).

Armstrong, Paul B., *The Phenomenology of Henry James* (Chapel Hill, 1983).

Esch, Deborah, '"Understanding Allegories": Reading *The Portrait of a Lady*', in *Henry James's The Portrait of a Lady* (ed.) Harold Bloom (New York, 1987).

Gilmore, Michael T., 'The Commodity World of *The Portrait of a Lady*', *New England Quarterly*, 59 (1986), pp. 51–74.

Habegger, Alfred, *Gender, Fantasy, and Realism in American Literature* (New York, 1982).

The Turn of the Screw (Part One)

12   Source criticism

Beidler, Peter, *Ghosts, Demons, and Henry James: The Turn of the Screw at the Turn of the Century* (Columbia, 1959).

Blackall, Jean Frantz, 'Cruikshank's *Oliver* and *The Turn of the Screw*', *American Literature*, 51 (1979), pp. 161–78.

Edel, Leon and Adeline R. Tintner, 'The Private Life of Peter Quin(t): Origins of "The Turn of the Screw"', *Henry James Review*, 6 (1985), pp. 2–4.

Lang, Hans-Joachim, 'The Turns in *The Turn of the Screw*', *Jahrbuch für Amerikastudien*, 9 (1964), pp. 110–28.

Nardin, Jane, '*The Turn of the Screw*: The Victorian Background', *Mosaic*, 12 (1978), pp. 131–42.

Petry, Alice Hall, 'Jamesian Parody, *Jane Eyre*, and 'The Turn of the Screw', *Modern Language Studies*, 13 (1983), pp. 61–78.

Roellinger, Francis X., Jr., 'Psychical Research and *The Turn of the Screw*', *American Literature*, 20 (1949), pp. 401–12.

Ryburn, May L., '*The Turn of the Screw* and *Amelia*: A Source for Quint?', *Studies in Short Fiction*, 16 (1979), pp. 235–7.

Scherero, Elliot M., 'Exposure in *The Turn of the Screw*', *Modern Philology*, 78 (1981), pp. 261–74.

Wolff, Robert Lee, 'The Genesis of *The Turn of the Screw*', *American Literature*, 13 (1941), pp. 1–8.

13   New criticism (apparitionist)

Evans, Oliver, 'James's Air of Evil: *The Turn of the Screw*', *Partisan Review*, 16 (1949), pp. 175–87; reprinted in *A Casebook on Henry James's 'The Turn of the Screw'* (ed.) Gerald Willen, 2nd ed. (New York, 1969), pp. 200–11.

Heilman, Robert, '*The Turn of the Screw* as Poem', *University of Kansas City Review*, 14 (1948); reprinted in *Casebook*.

Hoffman, Charles G., 'Innocence and Evil in James's *The Turn of the Screw*', *University of Kansas City Review*, 20 (1953), pp. 97–105; reprinted in *Casebook*, pp. 212–32.

Jones, Alexander E., 'Point of View in *The Turn of the Screw*', *Publications of the Modern Language Association*, 74 (1959), pp. 112–22; reprinted in *Casebook*, pp. 298–318.

14   Psychological criticism (non-apparitionist)

Aldrich, C. Knight, 'Another Twist to *The Turn of the Screw*', *Modern Fiction Studies*, 13 (1967), pp. 167–78; reprinted in *Casebook*, pp. 367–78.

Goddard, Harold C., 'A Pre-Freudian reading of *The Turn of the Screw*', *Nineteenth-Century Fiction*, 12 (June 1957), pp. 1–36; reprinted in *Casebook*, pp. 244–72.

Kenton, Edna, 'Henry James to the Ruminant Reader: *The Turn of the Screw*', *Arts*, 6 (1924), pp. 245–55; reprinted in *Casebook*, pp. 102–14.

Stepp, Walter, '*The Turn of the Screw*: If Douglas is Miles . . .', *Nassau Review*, 3 (1976), pp. 76–82.

West, Muriel, 'The Death of Miles in *The Turn of the Screw*', *Publications of the Modern Language Association*, 79 (1964), pp. 283–8; reprinted in *Casebook*, pp. 338–49.

Wilson, Edmund, 'The Ambiguity of Henry James', *Hound and Horn*, 7 (1934), pp. 385–406; reprinted in *Casebook*, pp. 115–53.

15   Post-new criticism

Felman, Shoshana, 'Turning the Screw of Interpretation', *Yale French Studies*, 55/56 (1977), pp. 225–40.

Mansell, Darrel, 'The Ghost in the Language of *The Turn of the Screw*', *Modern Language Quarterly*, 46 (1985), pp. 48–63.

Murphy, Kevin, 'The Unfixable Text: Bewilderment of Vision in *The Turn of the Screw*', *Texas Studies in Literature and Language*, 20 (1978), pp. 538–51.

Robbins, Bruce, 'Shooting Off James's Blanks: Theory, Politics, and *The Turn of the Screw*', *Henry James Review*, 5 (1984), pp. 192–9.

Siebers, Tobin, 'Hesitation, History, and Reading: Henry James's *The Turn of the Screw*', *Texas Studies in Literature and Language*, 25 (1983), pp. 558–73.

Other criticism

Auchincloss, Louis, 'A Strategy for James Readers', *The Nation*, 190 (April 23, 1960), pp. 364–7.

Barzun, Jacques, 'Henry James, Melodramatist', *Kenyon Review*, 5 (1943), pp. 508–21.

Berman, Paul, 'Down With the Modern Masters! French Theorists Dismember Things Past', *The Village Voice*, May 23, 1989, pp. 53–5.

Culver, Stuart, 'Representing the Author: Henry James, Intellectual Property and the Work of Writing', in *Henry James: Fiction as History* (ed.) Ian F. A. Bell (Totowa, 1985).

Guedalla, Philip, 'The Crowner's Quest', *The New Statesman*, 12 (February 15, 1919), pp. 421–2.

Kirby, David, *America's Hive of Honey, or Foreign Influences on American Fiction Through Henry James* (Metuchen, 1980).

Pirie, Gordon, *Henry James* (Totowa, 1974).

Seltzer, Mark, *Henry James and the Art of Power* (Ithaca, 1984).

Tintner, Adeline, '"High Melancholy and Sweet": James and the Arcadian Tradition', *Colby Library Quarterly*, 12 (1976), pp. 109–21.

Veeder, William, *Henry James – The Lesson of the Master: Popular Fiction and Personal Style in the Nineteenth Century* (Chicago, 1975).

Willen, Gerald (ed.) *A Casebook on Henry James's 'The Turn of the Screw'*, 2nd ed. (New York, 1969).

Index

Page numbers of main entries are indicated by boldface.